FEATURES

SPRING 2021•NUMBER 27

T0169581

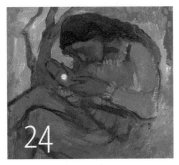

 Plough

DEPARTMENTS

WEB EXCLUSIVES

plough.com/web27

Plough
PLOUGH.COM

EDITOR: Peter Mommsen
SENIOR EDITORS: Maureen Swinger, Sam Hine, Susannah Black
EDITOR-AT-LARGE: Caitrin Keiper
MANAGING EDITOR: Maria Hine
POETRY EDITOR: A. M. Juster
DESIGNERS: Rosalind Stevenson, Miriam Burleson
CREATIVE DIRECTOR: Clare Stober
COPY EDITORS: Wilma Mommsen, Priscilla Jensen
FACT CHECKER: Suzanne Quinta
MARKETING DIRECTOR: Trevor Wiser
INTERNATIONAL EDITIONS: Ian Barth (UK), Kim Comer (German),
Chungyon Won (Korean), Allen Page (French)
CONTRIBUTING EDITORS: Joy Clarkson, Leah Libresco Sargeant,
Brandon McGinley, Jake Meador
FOUNDING EDITOR: Eberhard Arnold (1883–1935)

Plough Quarterly No. 27: The Violence of Love
Published by Plough Publishing House, ISBN 978-1-63608-034-5
Copyright © 2021 by Plough Publishing House. All rights reserved.

EDITORIAL OFFICE
151 Bowne Drive
Walden, NY 12586
T: 845.572.3455
info@plough.com

SUBSCRIBER SERVICES
PO Box 8542
Big Sandy, TX 75755
T: 800.521.8011
subscriptions@plough.com

United Kingdom
Brightling Road
Robertsbridge
TN32 5DR
T: +44(0)1580.883.344

Australia
4188 Gwydir Highway
Elsmore, NSW
2360 Australia
T: +61(0)2.6723.2213

Plough Quarterly (ISSN 2372-2584) is published quarterly by
Plough Publishing House, PO Box 398, Walden, NY 12586.
Individual subscription $32 / £24 / €28 per year.
Subscribers outside the United Kingdom and European Union pay in US dollars.
Periodicals postage paid at Walden, NY 12586 and at additional mailing offices.
POSTMASTER: Send address changes to
Plough Quarterly, PO Box 8542, Big Sandy, TX 75755.

Front cover and inside front cover: Francisco de Zurbarán, *Agnus Dei*, image
public domain. Back cover: Photograph by Albert Dros *(albertdros.com)*. Used
with permission.

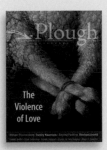

ABOUT THE COVER: The front cover art is
a detail from an *Agnus Dei* by the Spanish painter
Francisco de Zurbarán (1598-1664), depicting the
sacrificial Lamb of God (see John 1:29). The full
painting, which shows a merino lamb about one
year old, is shown on the inside front cover. Zurbarán
painted six versions of this image during his lifetime;
this version, widely considered his finest, was made
between 1635 and 1640, when he was working in
Seville. Oil on canvas, 15" by 24", Prado, Madrid.

Learning Generosity in Syria

Steve Gumaer

Mahmood's family with their newborn daughter, Loreen

I used to believe the fundamental premise of charity and compassion was material, that those who have more wealth than others share with those who lack. That we who are born into affluence, or inside functioning and privileged social structures, with opportunities to prosper, share with those who don't have the same chances. The rich give to the poor; the powerful give to the powerless.

Refugees and displaced people have obliterated this misconception.

In December 2019, I was in Al-Hasakah, in northeastern Syria, while the Turkish Armed Forces and their proxies continued an invasion of Kurdish Syria that had begun on October 9. Kurdish, Arab, and Armenian villages and cities along the border of Turkey were attacked, and people killed. Survivors fled into the desert or drove away in haste while roads were still unobstructed.

From that October until January 2020, my team and hundreds of volunteers

fed and provided for up to 27,000 people per day. The setting for all the aid we did was in primary schools and public buildings that were closed by the local administration to serve as temporary shelters until displacement camps could be established.

I visited one of those schools and went to a classroom where, I heard, a woman had just given birth to a beautiful girl. I was met at the door by a man with a big smile, earthy demeanor, farmer's hands. "I'm Mahmood," he said softly, employing the Middle Eastern gesture of smiling sincerely while resting his right hand over his heart. He pulled me into the classroom to join his wife and four children, including their newborn daughter, Loreen.

In a big circle on the floor, the family passed around a fragrant curry, rice, chili peppers, and flatbread. The best of every bowl was served onto my plate. Once everyone was served, through giggled whispers to each other, they gestured that I should begin my meal. With pantomime and the occasional translations of a friend, we heard their story as we shared a simple meal.

Mahmood, now grave, looked down at the floor as his kids cleared dishes. "We had just purchased doors and windows to finish our home. It's all gone." He strained to tell me that he and his family had saved for twenty years, building a home, piece by piece, as they could afford to from the meager income they earned as farmers.

Mahmood made space at his table for me, a stranger. He shared his family's food with me, selecting the best parts they had, filling my plate. His welcome – and his family's – was endearing and genuine, like that at so many meals I've shared with people in the Middle East.

I've learned from refugees and displaced people like Mahmood that charity isn't the responsibility or privilege of the wealthy alone, but all people, regardless of social or financial status, and it isn't practiced among the wealthiest people I know nearly as strikingly as with those I've known who are living in a state of material poverty and insecurity. For twenty-six years, I've been attempting to outdo victims of war with generosity, and so far, I've failed.

Do you want to experience hospitality? Go to any refugee camp or hide site for IDPs (internally displaced persons) in the world and be invited into the shack or tent of a family displaced by war, reduced to a few threadbare clothes, and some simple sentimental possessions like a wedding picture. You enter and a rush of activity ensues: water is boiled to make sweet tea. A meal is prepared. The table is wiped; a pillow is placed at the small of your back as they say, "Recline here. You must be so tired."

Material wealth may make generosity abundantly clear. But wealth is not required for generosity. One may be wealthy and generous but one may also be poor and generous. Wealth is a tool, and may as easily be employed falsely as altruistically.

In order to keep a lifeline of loving support working for families displaced by war, my team at Partners Relief & Development has had to be more creative and tenacious this year than ever before. With the challenges of bank failures, border closures, and all the new complexities created by the pandemic, some continue to press on with the imperative of loving action.

Those of us who have done this work for many years will tell you this: we learned the most important lessons of our labor from the people we set out to help. No matter the level of sacrifice or generosity, we will never outdo displaced families when it comes to intention, loving community, and sacrifice. We, like them, are learning to love by loving.

Poets in This Issue:

Catherine Tufariello lives in Oklahoma City. She is the author of *Keeping My Name*, which was awarded the Poets' Prize, and two chapbooks, *Annunciations* and *Free Time*. Her poems have appeared in *Able Muse Review, The Dark Horse, Literary Matters, Poetry,* and elsewhere. Read her poems on pages 23 and 87.

Rhina P. Espaillat is a bilingual poet who was born in the Dominican Republic and taught for decades in New York City public schools. She has won numerous prizes including the T. S. Eliot Prize, the Richard Wilbur Award, and (twice) the Howard Nemerov Sonnet award. Her most recent book is *Brief Accident of Light: Poems of Newburyport*, a collaboration with poet Alfred Nicol, with illustrations by artist Kate Sullivan (Kelsay Books, 2019). Read a selection of her poetry beginning on page 107.

Steve Gumaer and his wife, Oddny, founded Partners Relief & Development in 1994 as an international aid organization that works in war zones. Steve is Partners' president.

A Tireless Peacemaker

Lore Weber (1936–2020)

**Clemens Weber and
Chris Zimmerman**

Lore Weber on her eighty-fourth birthday in October 2020

"A slight, tender-hearted woman with boundless energy, always ready to help, to make peace, to comfort someone, or to stay up late writing yet another letter . . ." This is the Lore Weber described in an obituary after her death in Germany, in October 2020. She was eighty-four.

During her childhood, in a world awash in swastikas, guns, and fear, Lore developed a keen sense of justice and a deep hunger for peace.

In 1974, with her husband, Gerhard, a Lutheran pastor, she founded the Basisgemeinde, a "base community" modeled after the earliest Christian congregations. Its hallmarks included common housing, worship, work, and property, and a desire to publicly witness to justice and peace. In Gerhard's words, "To us, giving such a witness meant, first and foremost, trying to actually live out shalom – the peace of God." Both Gerhard and Lore stayed true to this calling, and to their fellow community members, through thick and thin. (And through years of poverty, marked most visibly by a diet centered around potatoes and whatever else could be grown in the community's garden.)

In 1990, the Webers founded a branch community in a rundown district of East Berlin. Arson threatened the new beginning (squatters had settled in the building and were not happy to see it being renovated and transformed), as did Gerhard's untimely death of cancer. Later, rising real estate values – the area became a hipster destination – emerged as the greatest threat to building up. Still, the little household dug in its heels, serving the homeless and the needy who came to their door, and welcoming children into the neighborhood kindergarten the community still runs.

To the end, Lore was tireless in her pursuit of peace and justice, both within her community and on a broader scale: in fighting for tenants' rights amid a rising tide of gentrification; as a board member of Church and Peace, a European ecumenical network; and more generally as a neighbor, in the biblical sense, to every person whose path crossed her own.

Asked what it means to work for justice and peace, Lore responded, "For years, I asked myself what I had to give or say to people in need – and I knew many! This self-questioning went on and on until, through an alcoholic, I found an answer that allowed me to stop torturing myself. She helped me see that I could simply be there, where such people were and are, and that by virtue of the simple fact that I believed in the unending love of God, I could have an effect on them, even without words." ⤵

Chris Zimmerman is a member of the Bruderhof and teaches at the Mount Academy in Esopus, New York. Clemens Weber, Lore Weber's son, is a member of the Basisgemeinde and lives in Berlin.

This Forum features selected responses to *Plough*'s Winter 2021 issue "What Are Families For?"; for a fuller conversation, please see the digital version at *Plough.com/Forum26*.

The Forum is a place for commissioned responses by other writers to the questions raised by our authors, and for letters from you, our readers. Send contributions to *letters@plough.com*, with your name and town or city; contributions may be edited for length and clarity, and may be published in any medium.

SINGLES IN CHURCH

On Gina Dalfonzo's "Singles in the Pew": I especially relate to this article on single people in the church. After twenty-four years of marriage, my former husband left me and our four teenage children. Suddenly, the church which had been at the center of our lives became a source of searing pain. Because my former husband and I were ministry leaders, the church was embarrassed and ashamed.

We were the victims of gossip, condemnation, and awkwardness. They didn't know what to do with us, visibly broken as we were, and the children and I no longer fit in with intact families.

If the church is to be a place for those who are broken, we must go the second mile to affirm, encourage, and include them. We need to look for creative ways to foster a sense of the family of God where the downtrodden can begin to heal. Our Father is faithful to his children, and the local church should be a reflection of him.

Rebecca Biegert Conti, Flagstaff, Arizona

Thank you for including this article under the topic of family – living one's life as a single is part of the whole picture; it is a reality for more than a few people. Gina Dalfonzo describes my own experience quite well. Even though I live among loving, caring families, the need to feel needed and the need for companionship are always there. I need encouragement and affirmation that a single life, lived for Christ and in his service, is a valid form of discipleship, just as those who are married need support and courage for marriage and parenting. As Christians, as brothers and sisters, we need each other; each person has something to give which another may need.

Judith Shirky, Rifton, New York

This is such a good reminder about why intentionality is important. I have been married for eight years and have one child and one on the way. But I was once single in the church as well. Presence was not automatic as it is for me

now, and it is far too easy for families to get wrapped up in our own chaos. But I know that there is room in our chaos for more of our church family.

Jeff Porter, St. Andrews, Scotland

THE CASE FOR BABIES

On Ross Douthat's "The Case for One More Child": Most people immediately throw out the possibility of having many kids and that's very sad. Yes, they're hard work; there are many days when I'm not sure how my husband or I get through with our sanity intact. I think a lot of people are underestimating themselves and don't want to give up their lifestyle. They sacrifice the betterment of the children and society for their own selfish desires. I'm not saying that applies to everyone, but I think it can be applied to most families with only one child. They value stuff, things, monetary comfort more than the expanse of life that comes with a large family. I grew up in a small family, and I now have five kids. I've seen both sides. I'll stand by my opinion.

Meghan Cherry
Dallas, Texas

What about the Christian's obligation to adopt? How does that play into big families, population, and contraception? (Adoptive parents are not all infertile, as is widely believed!) These kids are already here! Great points about kids decreasing selfish tendencies in parents; I try to tell my nulliparous friends this and they think I'm crazy!

Megan McManus
Raleigh, North Carolina

Yulia Brodskaya, *Feather*, paper quilling

The only solution to climate change is technology. Clean energy, geo-engineering, and carbon capture: the only way out is through. We need to become a rich and advanced enough society to be able to be proper stewards of the earth, and a growing population makes this easier. You only need to invent a technology once to spread it across the world, and the more people in rich countries, the more scientists and engineers we can support.

Mark Gilmour
Auckland, New Zealand

This article is thought-provoking, and I agree with Douthat's conclusion that we need a radical conversion of our hardened modern hearts, that siblings create the perfect first circle of socialization, and that parenting is one of the holiest callings of life.

With my husband I have parented birth, adoptive, and foster children. I am not sure that Douthat adequately addressed concerns of overpopulation, and I was surprised that he never raised the option of foster care. Overworked caseworkers in almost any state will happily fill your back seat. There will be considerably less temptation toward tribal narcissism and, when you are lucky, an expanded definition of extended family.

Mary Ann Conrad
Albuquerque, New Mexico

I loved two things about this article. The concept of children as a kind of everyman's sanctification is very relatable; second, I think this is applicable to everyone, not just people who are in faith and community traditions where there are large families already. My wife and I jointly probably would have settled on 0–1 kids as our ideal, but we now have two and I love them both dearly.

My main struggle is how to care for the aging previous generation when their ideal was paradoxical: sending their children to far-off regions of the United States for economic advancement and expecting us to move back in their later lives. I don't think that any of the articles in this issue addressed this other than to prescribe vague cultural ideals of accepting lower economic possibilities for the benefits of being closer to family.

Evan Leister
Kansas City, Missouri

TREASURE THE WEAK AND VULNERABLE

On Leah Libresco Sargeant's "Dependence": I have read and reread Leah Sargeant's essay about treasuring the weak and vulnerable. Thank you for this reminder to see human helplessness as God does! A verse from Zechariah 8 comes to mind: "Thus says the Lord of Hosts: Old men and old women shall again sit in the streets of Jerusalem, each one with his staff in his hand because of great age. The streets of the city shall be full of boys and girls playing in its streets." Contrast this with Hitler's vision for Germany: old, unproductive people cleared away to make room for workers in their prime while children are herded together and trained to become desirable citizens. But the true strength of a society lies in its care for the weak. God's holy city does not have streets cleared for commerce. The oldest and youngest citizens – those whose needs outbalance their productivity – are in the middle of everyday life. This is the real mark of a thriving city and a flourishing church, when the dependent are welcomed and celebrated.

Hannah Nisly
Altamont, Kansas

GOOD MASCULINITY

On Noah Van Niel's "Manly Virtues": I'm left with a big question: What distinguishes Van Niel's view of positive masculinity from a positive femininity? If Jesus is the role model for men, who is the role model for women? Are not all Christians meant to emulate Jesus, whatever their gender? Compassion, humility, and purpose: I have no argument with encouraging men to aspire to these virtues, but I see nothing essentially masculine in them. It seems to me that he is writing about "how to be truly human" (as one of the online comments on the article put it). I remain interested in the question of what does, or should, define a positive masculinity, and remain uncertain as to whether it is actually distinguishable from a positive femininity.

Jessamine Hyatt
Pittsboro, North Carolina

Noah Van Niel is right to seek a nuanced response to the "crisis of masculinity." For, as he says, many Christians respond by mixing the gospel with a defense of "traditional masculinity" that is not very Christian. But how should Christian men respond to the social changes behind the crisis? It is surely important to articulate a positive and hopeful response.

We have lived through a major cultural revolution. Because it is a matter of cultural politics rather than the governmental sort, its scale is easily overlooked. When my parents married, in the 1960s, both genders came in fairly firm cultural boxes. You had some freedom to move around in your box,

but you didn't think of leaving it any more than a tortoise thinks of leaving its shell. The old gender roles exaggerated the slight physical difference between men and women. Men were stronger in a wide sense – tougher, more worldly, more able to earn more money, and to think clearly. Women were softer, sillier, in need of protection. In the 1970s this set-up began to be seriously challenged, and then was overthrown. A shift this huge brings immense trauma as well as liberation and excitement – and most, but not all, of the trauma has fallen on men, robbed by feminism of their old aura of mastery.

I think that we should acknowledge this trauma, and also frame it in positive terms. That means acknowledging that the revolution was basically necessary and good. Those old boxes were bad for both sexes. They shaped us, but also constricted us. It also means seeing the resulting trauma as a process of painful growth and healing, a form of purgatory.

We should not drop our critical impulses – even good revolutions have sharp dangers. Van Niel wonders whether any blame lies with "the militant feminism that makes men feel like criminals before they do anything wrong." I think this slightly misses the point. The real dubious force of the revolution is not that it casts men in a negative light; the real danger is subtly different. We live in a culture of exaggeration, AKA idolatry – it doesn't know how to celebrate a morally virtuous movement without childishly pretending that it is divinely good, and that any perceived opposition is evil. And so, in our secular but not very rational age, feminism takes on a cultic aura; it implies that moral and spiritual significance resides in this gender rather than the other one. And this causes real and dangerous resentment.

Theo Hobson
London, England

BEYOND THE ENTRENCHED VIEW

On Sarah C. Williams's "The Praying Feminist": Josephine Butler's efforts remind me of the particular power of prayer to help us reimagine the world, ourselves and others, and our relationship with God, and move us beyond an entrenched and negative view of the world. I am also reminded of Ron Hansen's protagonist in *Mariette in Ecstasy* and her relationship with God: "We try to be formed and held and kept by him, but instead he offers us freedom. And now when I try to know his will, his kindness floods me, his great love overwhelms me, and I hear him whisper, Surprise me." God allows us to dream big, but how often do we take him up on his offer of freedom? It sounds like Josephine Butler did.

Father Michael Mayer
Rochester, New York ➤

John Wayne in the film *Hondo*, 1953

Turning a Corner

Amid the Pandemic, a Farm Stand Is Born

MAUREEN SWINGER

COLEMAN CORNERS was dreamed up on a steep mountain road in a February snowstorm. "Who's he?" you might ask, followed by "Why were you out in a storm?" The truth is, Coleman is a little farm stand, and also a centerpoint for sanity, and my husband and I were having wild ideas in the wilderness because the storm and the high roads were gifting us with six rare, uninterrupted hours to talk.

From Fox Hill Bruderhof, we'd deserted our three kids (responsibly) to surprise a good friend who had seen us through a tough time and then moved too far away. We wcre mounting a stealth raid with a massive birthday basket, silly hats, and an even sillier song with which to barge through the front door.

The barge was a joyous success – just a few hours of celebration, laughter, and true talk, fueling the energy cells for what we didn't know the year would bring. Then we had to hit the road home, looking forward to hugging the three livewires at the other end, while still glad they were not in the back seat.

"So the old Coleman House finally came down . . ." mused Jason, as our wheels clung to another mountain curve. "What can we do with a location so close to a big road, with such a beautiful view, and its own drive?"

Coleman's was an ancient farmhouse on the

Maureen Swinger is an editor at Plough *and lives at the Fox Hill Bruderhof in Walden, New York, with her husband, Jason, and their three children.*

corner of our Fox Hill property; last fall it had succumbed to time, rot, and a demolition team.

"What about a little farm stand? A cozy spot off Coleman Road with a play area for kids?"

"Yeah, and a chill area for parents . . . with Adirondack chairs . . ."

"We could turn around the funds for local shelters or food pantries, or if someone needs a wheelchair ramp . . ."

The idea was met with approval from the rest of the Fox Hill folk, providing we could build and run the thing in our spare time. "Spare time" is ephemeral on a busy community, so we started collecting materials and sketching plans for a shed and surroundings to be finished in a year or two. Then the whole world shut down, and something as frivolous as a farm stand seemed ridiculous in New York, for a while the epicenter of a pandemic. We were worried out of our minds for distant friends, I was homeschooling those three livewires, and Jay – Jay was *not* working.

Home-free is not a happy thing for a builder, unless he can park his carpentry trailer in the backyard and build something there. But what? Perhaps a post-and-beam farm stand. Could a son finish his math faster if he got to go out to hammer and chisel after? He could. Though we now had the time to build it, when would it ever see use, in this strange stay-at-home era?

Turns out, much sooner than we thought. Framed out in July, and forklifted onto a flatbed, the little shed traveled slowly to its hilltop location. Jay finished siding it by sunrise light. A few families joined us to clear brambles and burn brush, sow grass and start a small playground under a big maple.

In August, our garden was booming. We posted our first tentative Facebook event for a Saturday afternoon, promising an open-air farmers' market and asking folks to wear masks and give each other space. Privately, I

thought we'd have more than enough space between the two or three old friends who would come so as not to leave us hanging.

One hundred and twenty people showed up over four hours. Everyone wore a mask. No one crowded anyone else. We ran out of sweet corn and cucumbers. But more than vegetables, people wanted voices. They stood around in spacious circles and talked. "How've you been?" "You surviving the summer?" "Have you heard if Joe and Linda are doing all right?" "They've been hit hard." "We're praying." "I'm taking them some of this fresh bread and tomatoes."

The next Saturday, we had more chairs, set up in decorously distant circles under the trees. More people came. Even though the farm-stand side of it did almost frantic business, it felt more like a peaceable festival – the chairs were full of people, chatting and laughing across the six-foot spaces. Our friend Mark's booming laugh could wrap around the whole circle, especially when the walnut tree started to bomb us. Or maybe it was his laugh that shook the nuts down.

> **We ran out of sweet corn and cucumbers. But more than vegetables, people wanted voices.**

Two ladies from Walden came every week, bringing their mothers, making an afternoon of it. The matriarchs sat, still and queenly in their wheelchairs, reigning over their circles while their daughters chatted and shopped. As they rolled out, one leaned over and whispered, "This is my church!" Another elderly lady told us her greatest fear wasn't Covid, but loneliness: "I don't even know anyone to call and talk to. There's nowhere to go to see a face that's not on TV. I can't take one more day on my own."

> **This place was born out of a determination to defy distance and celebrate face to face.**

Among our staff, talents surprised us as Farmstand Saturday became a glowing beacon on the calendar. Our daughter mastered the cash register. Our son rigged the lawn tractor to haul large loads of pumpkins. Three little cousins got professional at popping up tents, labeling bins, crating eggs. Our friend Barb, a brilliant musician who missed her local orchestra and chamber groups, invited all the area musicians to reconnect and talk shop over the pastry table.

Speaking of pastries, Edna, a legendary Fox Hill baker, worked ahead each week to make apple pies and Danish that always disappeared within the first half hour. She has never managed to make any quantity to outlast that timeframe. Edna is seventy-six. Her older sister Emma had laid down her paintbrushes a few years ago, saying no one was really interested in her kind of art anymore. But she picked up her exquisite stone and driftwood sculpture work again when we started displaying home-made crafts. Now we can't keep her owls on the shelves. The kids stand in front of them to see if they'll blink. There are folks making pottery and home decorations. It's a whirling flurry of industry.

Could we use more staff? Probably. Does my house ever get cleaned? Ehhh. Is it worth all the scramble? I'd have to give that an unequivocal yes. Every time I look over this sloping little meadow, alive with people, I think back to the way Coleman Corners came about. Much of the last year has been a war waged against encroaching walls, silence, and a fear beyond illness – a fear of being alone, living alone, dying alone. It makes sense that this place was born out of a determination to defy distance and celebrate face to face.

See you up at the Corners for maple-sapping season! ⬿

Watch the Coleman Corners story:
Plough.com/Coleman

Can Violence Be Good?

Meekness and Its Discontents

PETER MOMMSEN

FROM ALL THE LOSSES of the last year, with its countless ordeals and heartbreaks, let's pick out one that may seem an abstraction. It's the loss of a once-sturdy taboo. At some point between George Floyd's killing on May 25 and the invasion of the US Capitol on January 6, our culture's consensus against political violence crumbled. Before 2020, we lived in a society that (except for its left and right fringes) overwhelmingly agreed that using violence for political ends ought to be out of bounds. Now, we know that many of our fellow citizens are sort-of-OK with violence – at least when it's their own side that is breaking windows and punching police officers.

Like any generalization, this statement needs lots of hedges. Most obviously, the now-broken taboo against political violence was always selectively applied; too often, it was a norm imposed on some but not others, as the history of Jim Crow shows. In addition, it's not obvious why the violence of a riot should be condemned more harshly than other kinds of violence that, though less dramatic, are more deadly. The US prison system, for example, through its willful negligence in providing medical care, takes far more lives each year than any hotheaded protest; so does the abortion industry. And that is to leave to the side for the moment the matter of foreign wars or of Western complicity in China's concentration camps for Uighurs.

We also don't know if the suspension of the taboo against violence will prove to be temporary, just one more passing symptom of the feverish months of the pandemic. Perhaps the anti-violence consensus will reemerge once the order of ordinary life is more or less restored.

Perhaps. Yet even when we've made all the necessary hedges, something significant seems to have slipped. The old taboo was bound up with a bundle of ideals: civility in disagreement, respect for the rule of law, peaceful transfers of power. It found expression in the civic religion of Martin Luther King Day, with its irenic "I Have a Dream" universalism. Its emotional power came from a vague but broadly shared conviction that the arc of the universe really does bend toward justice.

It's hard to see how this old mythology, whose hold had weakened long before 2020, can easily be restored to its former power. This was obvious, for example, during last summer's Black Lives Matter protests. While downtown Minneapolis burned, journalists sympathetic to the protests joined in chorus to repeat Reverend King's line about riots being the "language of the unheard." But many fell strangely silent when it came to King's uncompromising belief in nonviolence (and not unrelatedly,

In medieval bestiaries, the mother pelican is a symbol of self-sacrifice, impaling herself to feed her young. Illustration for *Plough* by Rudolf Koch, 1923.

his Christianity). In fact, *nonviolence* seemed to have become a dirty word among certain progressives; even while quoting King, they clearly yearned for Stokely Carmichael, or maybe Frantz Fanon.

On the right, this kind of doublespeak occasioned much hooting about the "mostly peaceful protesters." But of course the most spectacular recent act of political violence did not come from the left. 2020 was the year when the Proud Boys and Oath Keepers and their ilk were ramping up for their own "mostly peaceful" protest in Washington, DC.

I S THERE ANY WAY BACK to a broad agreement that violence is wrong? Since this is a Christian magazine, it is only right to begin by taking stock of our own house, asking what guilt we Christians bear in political violence, and what counterprogram Christianity ought to be offering. Answering those questions is obviously beyond the scope of this brief article. But two points seem important to touch on.

The first is the rise of so-called Christian nationalism as a conspicuous player in the political violence of the past months, not least in the attack on the US Capitol. This movement combines exhibitionist public prayer and "Jesus 2020" banners with strong elements of White supremacism and a readiness for lethal violence.

All this, it should go without saying, is not Christian, even if this movement historically has deep roots in White American Christian culture. The disconnect shows up most blatantly when so-called Christian nationalists take the symbol of the cross – the sign of an executed Jew who refused to defend himself – and turn it into a badge for a semiautomatic-toting tribalism. It's hard to imagine anything more alien to the way of the Jesus of the Gospels.

This brings us to the second point: What might a truly Christian stance look like? One place to begin is a text so overfamiliar that it can feel irrelevant: the Beatitudes, with their blessings on the peacemakers, the merciful, and the meek.

Among these Beatitudes, meekness is easily the least popular. But perhaps for just that reason, it's the most necessary today. It's hardly coincidental that a society in which political violence is increasing is also a society that despises meekness. Ours is a moment proud of its us-versus-them realism; it delights in shaming enemies and relishes the obliterating smackdown. This habit of mind extends across the left–right spectrum to both critical race theorists and integralist theocons. If what matters is the contest for raw power, then coercion is a necessary tool.

As for meekness, this worldview is pretty well its opposite. Yet the Beatitude must apply even in times of conflict, or it doesn't apply at all. When read in the context of the Sermon on the Mount as a whole, Jesus' call to meekness isn't merely about being amiable in private life. He plainly intends us to practice meekness in extreme situations, when doing so seems to violate all norms of justice: When someone hits you, turn your face for a second blow. When forced to go one mile, volunteer for a second. When someone demands your coat, give him your shirt as well. Forgive not just forgivable wrongs, but the wrongs that seem unforgivable.

Such meekness goes beyond self-abnegation. It is generous. (Thomas Aquinas highlighted this by linking the virtue of meekness to the virtue of magnanimity.) Without a willingness to yield to others, it's impossible to give them the benefit of the doubt, grant them a second chance, show them mercy – in short, to love them as oneself.

You have heard that it was said, "You shall love your neighbor and hate your enemy." But I say to you, Love your enemies and pray for those who persecute you, so that you may be sons of your Father who is in heaven; for he makes his sun rise on the evil and on the good, and sends rain on the just and on the unjust. (Matt. 5:43–45)

This call to love even one's enemy shows the Christian approach not just to political violence, but to violence in general. If I love my enemy, I cannot harbor rage against him. If I love my enemy, I cannot join a predatory Twitter mob to cancel him (even when I must vocally disagree with him). If I love my enemy, I cannot wish to see him harmed or dead – and I certainly cannot kill him.

WHILE CHRISTIANS over the centuries have always honored nonviolence, they have often interpreted it as a supernatural ideal. The result is that nonviolence is cast as a special calling that depends on others, the non-nonviolent, to do the dirty work: defending the vulnerable, keeping the public peace, and protecting the nonviolent themselves from the bad guys.

If this were so, nonviolence would amount to the worst spiritual selfishness (as Reinhold Niebuhr and others have charged). But that's not how the Sermon on the Mount sees it. Here in Christianity's preeminent teaching, nonviolence is just one prosaic, even obvious, expression of a new way of life. It's a life that is to be wholly reshaped by the unstinting generosity of perfect love: "You, therefore, must be perfect, as your heavenly Father is perfect" (Matt. 5:48).

If we take Jesus' call to nonviolence at face value, we're left with all kinds of interesting practical questions: What about policing? What about the military? What about participating in government? Some, but by no means all, of these questions are addressed in the pages that follow. It's not our aim here to propose a neat system of ethical rules about nonviolence – to "set up a new theoretical orthodoxy," as Eberhard Arnold puts it (page 31). Any such attempt would be untrue to the Sermon on the Mount's own generosity. Instead, this issue of *Plough* aims only to explore what a life lived according to love rather than violence might look like.

In 1977, the archbishop of San Salvador, Oscar Romero, was locked in confrontation with El Salvador's oligarchical government after criticizing its bloody repression of popular protests. Romero, in turn, was accused of preaching revolutionary violence. He denied this: "We have never preached violence, except the violence of love, which left Christ nailed to a cross." He returned to this theme in a 1979 address:

> The only violence that the gospel admits is violence to oneself. When Christ lets himself be killed, that is violence – letting oneself be killed. Violence to oneself is more effective than violence to others. It is very easy to kill, especially when one has weapons, but how hard it is to let oneself be killed for love of the people!

Romero knew what might well be coming his way. Seven months later, he was shot by a right-wing assassin while saying Mass.

The meekness Romero lived and died for seems nonsensical from a realist point of view. In utilitarian terms, martyrdom will always seem nonsensical. The Beatitudes may promise that the meek will inherit the earth. But human history seems a massive refutation of the idea that the meek will inherit anything at all.

Unless, that is, what the Gospels tell about Easter is true: that a meek victim rose bodily from the dead and now rules as lord of the universe. If that is true, then the answer to violence becomes plain. It begins and ends with the violence of self-sacrificial love. ⤳

ANTHONY M. BARR

With Love
We Shall Force
Our Brothers

Prophetic Peacemaking with James Baldwin

W**HEN I WAS A LITTLE BOY,** I had two answers to "What do you want to be when you grow up?" A preacher, I said, or a police officer. Sometimes I said I would be both. Both aspirations lasted for perhaps as much as a decade of my life.

Neither occupation runs in my family, nor did I have specific childhood idols to entice me toward such seemingly disparate careers. If I had to guess why they both appealed, it was probably my abiding sense of justice. A pastor might offer insight on managing your temper, but a preacher rails against social sins, and a cop, well, a cop catches bad guys.

Growing up an American Evangelical, from time to time I took those "spiritual gifts" inventory tests, strange mixtures of pop psychology and biblical exegesis inspired by Saint Paul's letter to the church in Corinth. The results tended to be consistent: they said I have the gift of prophecy. As a kid, I thought prophecy was about predicting the future, or standing against the Antichrist in the End Times.

But the Old Testament prophets didn't really do a lot of predicting. Instead, they spoke out against social sins, political sins, the sins of empire, the evils of a regime that turns its back on God and exploits and oppresses the poor and marginalized, a state that perpetuates injustice. The more I read the Old Testament, the more my perspective shifted. A prophetic preacher advocates for the innocent with burning indignation, and a cop, well, a cop catches bad guys.

By my mid-teens, those aspirations had faded. Now I wanted to be a filmmaker; I was in love with the idea of transforming the culture through storytelling that would rival the best of Hollywood's. Anyway, the whole idea of a career in law enforcement had run up against my own interiority, especially the persistent sense that I could never pursue a career that required me to carry a gun. Sometimes a cop has to kill the bad guy, I reasoned. I knew I could never do it.

Ferguson was the moment when all my tidy narratives about justice unraveled. In 2014, Officer Darren Wilson shot and killed Michael Brown, age eighteen, and then city officials left his body in the street for four hours. Ferguson was the moment when I could not turn from what I had only just begun to understand, that so many cops across this nation look at Black bodies like my own and describe them as demons. I would later read the Justice Department report that painstakingly documented how Ferguson used aggressive policing and civil forfeiture law as an explicit profit-maximizing scheme for the city government. And I would do a deep dive into the history of police brutality and the rise of the carceral state as a new Jim Crow regime. My freshman year of college, I would work with Dr. Anthony Bradley on his book on ending

Alfred Conteh, *Will*, charcoal, acrylic, and atomized bronze dust on paper

---

Anthony M. Barr, a graduate student at Pepperdine University, has written for the American Conservative *and the* University Bookman. *He is an editor for the Pepperdine School of Public Policy's "The American Project," which promotes a communitarian conservatism.*

overcriminalization and mass incarceration. But before all that studying, before I had positioned my intuitions within a conceptual framework, it was the lifeless body of Michael Brown, discarded in the middle of a public street, that pierced me.

Peacemaking is intrinsically tied to solidarity with whomever one's regime is presently nailing to a cross.

In the aftermath of Ferguson, my relationship with Evangelicalism unraveled too, and with it any last vestiges of wanting to be a preacher. The discourse surrounding policing in America marked a line in the sand, dividing those who celebrate what they call the vindication of rule of law from those who understand the suffering of my people. Jesus didn't die to protect your house in the suburbs, I argued again and again with White Evangelicals who quoted the Book of Romans to justify state violence. And so I revised my mental categories again: a pastor proclaims "a year of plenty" for God's favorite White middle-class Christians; a prophet is just another "angry black man" and made to feel unwelcome in his hometown; and a cop, well, a cop is someone employed by the state to kill with impunity.

Between the World and Me

In 2015, Ta-Nehisi Coates's book *Between the World and Me* hit my heart with the force of a hurricane. In its pages I found political anger: not the usual faux outrage of performative populism but concentrated rage, undiluted and unapologetic. And here I found a testament to the body as the place where the forces of the world and every aspiration we could ever have

intersect. *Between the World and Me* is written as a letter from a father to his son, a letter about what it means to live in a world where your very body is perceived as a threat, where the physical appearance of your skin, your eyes, your hair invites violence.

Coates's words seared me: "But all our phrasing – race relations, racial chasm, racial justice, racial profiling, white privilege, even white supremacy – serves to obscure that racism is a visceral experience, that it dislodges brains, blocks airways, rips muscle, extracts organs, cracks bones, breaks teeth." Coates charges his son, and all his readers, never to "look away from this."

Coates has no room in his worldview for religion, in particular none for an Old Man in the Sky who is forever assuring a justice that is always deferred. Promised peace in a picturesque afterlife is not much of a balm for those suffering unjust miseries now. Your body is all you have, Coates tells his son, so make sure you guard it well. The follow-up to his debut is a book called *We Were Eight Years in Power*; for Coates, power, especially Black power, is all that separates bodies – his, his son's, mine – from the skull-crushing force of a social world that is hostile to people like us.

Coates is not the first Black person to reject religion and its metaphysics of hope as an inadequate response to White violence. This tradition fueled some of the most important work in civil rights, such as the way that the Black Panthers were able to feed, clothe, and educate their own in self-determining communities.

But Coates is wrong about religion. What he misses is the profound solidarity at the heart of the gospel, the world-altering reality that when we say "body, broken for you," we mean a literal broken body, and that this literal broken body is given for him, and you, and me. Jesus

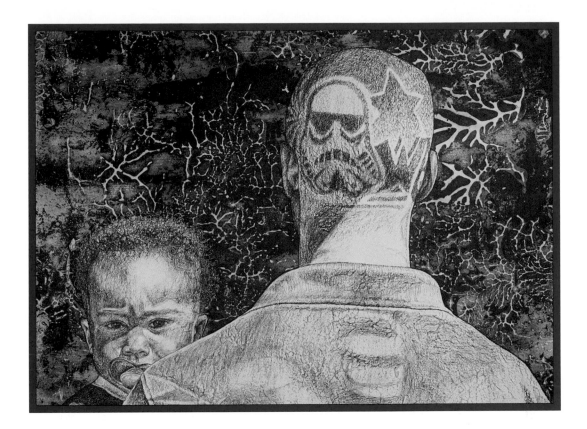

has placed his body between our bodies and the world. It is the nexus where suffering meets grace, where oppression gives way to radical self-emptying. The table at which he offers us his body is a place of egalitarianism where one's race and social station have no weight or meaning. It is also a place of inescapable solidarity, for it is here that we are united to Christ's cross, here that we are empowered to bear our crosses and so fill up in our own flesh the redemptive suffering of Christ, as Paul writes to the Colossians.

Peace, but Not Quiet

"Blessed are the peacemakers, for they shall be called sons of God."

What does it mean that Christ, the Prince of Peace who "bears the weight of the government on his shoulder," invites us into the work of peacemaking? What does it mean that Christ,

the only-begotten Son of God, connects peace-making to sharing in sonship?

I believe we cannot fully understand these teachings without understanding that Christ crucified is Christ executed unjustly by an oppressive political regime. When we confess in the creed that he was crucified "under Pontius Pilate," it is important that we say "under" and not "by." It is not simply that Christ is killed by unjust men; he is killed under the sanction of political authority as the direct outcome of an explicitly political process which includes a procedural trial and a judicial sentencing.

This is to say that whatever the work of peacemaking is, it cannot be thought of as simply maintaining the "rule of law" of whatever regime holds political power. The path of peacemaking is altogether different than the one that leads to mere good citizenship or

Alfred Conteh, *Triple E and His Daddy*, charcoal, acrylic, and atomized steel dust on paper

Alfred
Conteh,
Atlas,
charcoal and
acrylic on
paper

the preservation of a polity. Indeed, if peace-making involves emulating the Prince of Peace who bears the government on his shoulder as whip scars and a wooden cross, it's clear that peacemaking is intrinsically tied to solidarity with whomever one's regime is presently nailing to a cross. The justice of Christ's cross is a justice of reconciliation, a pathway to peace for those who have been denied it.

There are those who preach that to focus on ending wrongs in the here and now betrays the integrity of Christ's message. But that confuses the genuine insight that Christ's kingdom is not worldly – that it is attached to no earthly regime – with the idea that God is indifferent to the injustices of our present moment. God

was not indifferent to the blood of Abel that cried out to him from the ground; God was not indifferent to the husbands denounced by Malachi, who forsook their marriage vows; and Jesus was certainly not indifferent to the moneychangers in the temple who exploited the common people.

The fundamental purpose of God's prophets, then, is to make peace by calling us to the repentance that leads to reconciliation and by simultaneously advocating for the material and social conditions that make peace possible. And I think that the reason prophets run up against civil authorities so consistently is precisely because the work of creating peace requires confrontation with the forces that undermine peace through exploitation and violence. Peace is not the same thing as quiet.

Reading Baldwin

The great Black humanist James Baldwin foreshadows some of the themes of Coates's book; he even couches some of them in a letter to a relative. Published in 1962, Baldwin's heartbreaking "A Letter to My Nephew" is situated against the backdrop of profound racial injustice that assailed him and led to his expatriation as a young man.

Baldwin's letter begins by describing the kind of intimate relationship he had with his brother, the father of his nephew. "I don't know if you have known anybody from that far back, if you have loved anybody that long, first as an infant, then as a child, then as a man," writes Baldwin, but in doing so "you gain a strange perspective on time and human pain and effort." This context is important because it bolsters Baldwin's authority to speak into the life of his nephew – as he says, "I know the conditions under which you were born for I was there."

Baldwin and Coates both understand that loving people who suffer from the cruelty of others shapes your perspective on the world and your relationship to others. Baldwin writes, "I know what the world has done to my brother and how narrowly he has survived it and I know, which is much worse, and this is the crime of which I accuse my country and my countrymen and for which neither I nor time nor history will ever forgive them, that they have destroyed and are destroying hundreds of thousands of lives and do not know it and do not want to know it."

This is the great obstacle to all peacemaking: the subtle defense mechanisms we use to preserve not knowing. So the work of peacemaking is always prophetic; it requires

us to see in order to act. Throughout scripture the prophetic word calls God's people toward recognition of, and repentance for, collective and individual wrongdoing. This is the prerequisite for the concrete action required to establish a right relationship with God and neighbor, between ruler and ruled, and within the family – to begin to create social justice.

But how do we get there? How do we adopt a right posture toward a world that hurts us, toward people who demean and devalue us, toward the kind of visceral violence that leads

---

This is the great obstacle to all peacemaking: the subtle defense mechanisms we use to preserve not knowing.

---

to a lifeless body lying on asphalt in a public street for four August hours? Here Baldwin's letter challenges us again. First, he charges his nephew with the task of accepting those who oppress him in willful ignorance and false innocence. He writes: "You must accept them and accept them with love, for these innocent people have no other hope. They are in effect still trapped in a history which they do not understand and until they understand it, they cannot be released from it."

Nevertheless, it is not enough simply to accept. For everyone's sake, oppressor and oppressed, it is not nearly enough. Baldwin adds an even weightier task. He writes that "we with love shall force our brothers to see themselves as they are, to cease fleeing from reality and begin to change it." This is a defiance every bit as strong as Coates's, but it is rooted in a much more expansive love. The love of the peacemaker is a love that has force, that will

Alfred Conteh, *Crishelle,* charcoal, acrylic, and atomized steel dust on paper

not accept the injustices of the status quo, that will not allow the willful ignorance of those who oppress to drown out the prophetic word and the reconciliation and peace that is offered to all of us through Christ's cross.

I am still trying to learn about love from Baldwin, still trying to figure out how to reconcile deep hurt with acceptance, still trying to figure out how to bear the cross of solidarity in such a way as to enable peace. I don't think that most people are racist, I don't think that most cops are killers, and I don't think that the miscarriages of justice in our nation are a sign that it is beyond all hope. I respect power, and I believe in its efficacy, but I don't believe that

power is all we have or that it is a greater force in the world than love.

I'm in graduate school now, studying public policy. I still dream of helping to make the world a better place. Maybe that was the underlying thread of my childhood aspirations, of which justice is one vital piece. Maybe in a roundabout way, it has always been about love. I'll let Baldwin have the last word: "We have not stopped trembling yet, but if we had not loved each other, none of us would have survived, and now you must survive because we love you and for the sake of your children and your children's children." ➤

March Thaw

Overhead, skeins of geese *ya-honk* as they pass.
The dwindling snow crust, an eggshell of glass,
Cracks underfoot, hatching tufts of pale grass,

And the air smells of loam and ozone. Sumps brim
And windows creak open; each twig wears a scrim
Of blurred buds, and the weather's new watchword is *Whim*.

Who'd have guessed that all winter, white dreamed of green?
That icicles burned to catch fire? The pristine,
Marmoreal palace of grief, the White Queen,

Starts to shimmer and swim. Once numb with despair,
Her ice statues glisten, with bright, dripping hair
And tears in their eyes. Look, touch the one there,

The cold stone of her hand. Feel it soften. Consent
To let her draw breath. Let perfection relent.
Wind loves the branches, though blemished and bent.

Let the child's tugging kite take flight from the park,
Let seed leaves emerge from the nourishing dark,
Let sap find its way to the tap in the bark.

CATHERINE TUFARIELLO

J. Kirk Richards, *A Pearl of Great Price*

The *Risk* of Gentleness

Welcoming the Baby I Did Not Want

GRACY OLMSTEAD

A LIMB SKIMMED THE INSIDE of my belly, the slick slide of it like a marble rolling underneath my skin. A tiny baby boy jostled my insides, engaging in his regular evening ritual of chaotic movement. I sat feeling his unknown shape bump up against my own, considering all this child's unknowns: the thickness of his hair, the hue of his eyes, the shape of his nose. Closer than a brother, yet more mysterious than a stranger.

This is the child I did not expect. He is the child I would have told you, a year ago, I did not want. But his story, like so many, is bound up in the mysterious timeliness of a God who seems to enjoy astonishing us. As I sat – nine months pregnant – during Advent, surrounded by reminders of Jesus' imminent birth, I found myself dwelling often on the sacred surprises we neither expect nor fully deserve. In 2020, like many others, I realized how often love calls us to take frightful, beautiful risks.

Gracy Olmstead is a journalist whose writing has appeared in the American Conservative, *the* Week, *the* New York Times, *and the* Washington Post, *among others. Her book* Uprooted: Recovering the Legacy of the Places We've Left Behind *will be released on March 16, 2021.*

J. Kirk Richards, *Mother and Child*, unfinished

I

T WAS A SATURDAY MORNING, the week after Easter. I woke up knowing that I was pregnant. The reality of it had settled under my eyelids sometime during the night, and solidified by the time I fully awoke. I knew there was a baby inside me – even though my fertility planning app would have suggested such a thing to be out of the question.

While our toddler girls burst into our room, jumped onto the bed, and tickled their daddy awake, I slipped downstairs. I rummaged around the bathroom cupboard for the pregnancy test that was jammed into a back corner. The result itself was an afterthought: proof to show the rest of the world. I wasn't surprised by its answer. I carried the test up to my husband, showed him the positive sign, and burst into tears.

I was ashamed, as a pro-life Christian, to feel this mixture of fear and stress upon discovering I was pregnant. I believed with all my heart that each life was precious. So many women never get to be mothers. I knew I was supposed to feel unadulterated joy in this new life. But I was also weary. 2019 was the sort of year that compelled me to beg with God for a respite in 2020 – a break from the emotional, physical, financial, and familial crises that had filled so many of our days. Yet here we were, four months into the year, navigating the unknowns of a worldwide pandemic. My husband was still required to commute to work every day, while I sheltered in place with two busy little girls, trying to meet deadlines and simultaneously keep them happy. We had been losing internet service and running water intermittently for the past several weeks, while my almost-two-year-old had developed a knack for danger and mischief that left me in a state of vigilant panic. There was no room, I felt, for more. No room to hold another life, its combined challenges and joys.

I knew I would choose this baby, say yes to him, despite my fears and exhaustion. There was never any doubt in my mind that this baby was ours, and that he was a gift to us. But I also

J. Kirk Richards, *Mother and Child*, unfinished

knew that I was choosing him, in those early days, despite myself.

There's a tendency in some pro-life Christian circles to fear acknowledging the difficulty in choosing life. But this closes us off to the love and empathy we must extend to women who truly need it. We dismiss their hurts, difficulties, and anxieties far too easily. I was reminded that day in April (and have been reminded many days since) of the women whose life circumstances are far harder than any I have experienced, for whom poverty, single mother-hood, an abusive spouse, or a life-threatening condition make pregnancy frightening and perilous. I was reminded of how easy it is, as a pro-life person, to ignore or excuse the difficulty of embracing this unseen life.

But the truth of choosing life is that it nec-essarily involves embracing risk and fear. In a world that suggests we ought to be in control, or that we can *make* control for ourselves, pregnancy and parenting confront us with a whole slew of uncontrollable, unknowable realities. Contrary to popular slogans, parenthood cannot be planned. Sometimes the vestige of control is shattered in a relatively gentle way: when labor does not arrive when we thought, or the supposedly "simple" work of breastfeeding mystifies us and shatters our maternal confidence. Sometimes it takes a more tragic turn: in the heart condition discovered prior to birth, the child lost to SIDS, the grown daughter or son who struggles with addiction. Regardless, parenting requires us to make space for more than we think we can. It is a form of radical hospitality, and pregnancy turns this reality, this stretching in order to make room, into an embodied metaphor we mothers inhabit for nine months.

Embracing a new life requires more than passive acceptance. It is true that our bodies begin the process of preparation before our minds and emotions even register what is happening. But once the reality of another life is impressed upon the mind, another work must happen. Soul and mind reach forward

J. Kirk Richards, *Mother and Child*

into the darkness, the unknown, and make room where there appears to be none in an imaginative work of hospitality that begins bodily, but extends into every crevice of life.

"They know and feel, that the *potential* works *in* them, even as the *actual* works on them!" wrote Coleridge of both philosophers and caterpillars, comparing the inquisitive imagination to that "instinct" which impels the chrysalis to leave room for antennae yet to come.

This tension between the potential and the actual, making space through expectation and faith, is in fact a very apt description of the work to become a mother. Preparing room for a child can often appear to be a passive experience, letting the body take over. But it is what the late philosopher Anne Dufourmantelle called an "active passivity": one in which gentleness becomes subversive and radical through its determined and resolute nature.

As THE MONTHS of my pregnancy passed, I thought often of the Virgin Mary, of the powerful gentleness which characterized her motherhood and her life. No other woman knows more fully what it means to cultivate a free and open hospitality to the mysterious, beautiful child within. In her simple yet radical obedience – her words "Let it be to me according to your word" – active passivity takes on new meaning and potency.

"This is precisely her greatest glory: that having nothing of her own, retaining nothing of a 'self' that could glory in anything for her own sake, she placed no obstacle to the mercy of God and in no way resisted His love and His will," writes the Trappist monk Thomas Merton. In Mary's revolutionary act of hospitality, God's will and liberty were "in no way hindered or turned from [their] purpose by the presence of an egotistical self." She watched and waited, embraced the risk and fear of a broken world – one which would assail her and her son, time and time again – and showed us a pattern of loving welcome.

Dufourmantelle writes in *Power of Gentleness* (2018) that every act of human caregiving is bound up in gentleness's active passivity and determination to make space. Through powerful gentleness, we embrace the fragility and singularity of the other. But gentleness is also a form of caring distance, of making "way for what is most singular in others" – seeing them as they *are*, rather than merely as we want them to be.

Hospitality "means primarily the creation of a free space where the stranger can enter and become a friend instead of an enemy," writes Henri J. M. Nouwen in *Reaching Out: The Three Movements of the Spiritual Life* (1975). "Hospitality is not to change people, but to offer them space where change can take place. It is not to bring men and women over to our side, but to offer freedom not disturbed by dividing lines." No matter how well known the other may be, it is ultimately the act of one mysterious soul reaching out to another – which requires us to respect the distance and freedom of the other. Though "empty space tends to create fear," he writes, "the paradox of hospitality is that it wants to create emptiness, not a fearful emptiness, but a friendly emptiness where strangers can enter and discover themselves as created free."

In 2020, I felt more sharply the distance and mystery which exists between human persons: the divergence of opinion and experience, geography and belief, flesh and spirit. But with every new month of challenge and heartbreak, something in me responded by softening and stretching yet a little bit more. It was not a perfect process: all too often, I gave in to fury and petulance, pride and vanity. But from the

> We fear God's blessings more often than we ask for them, and seek to substitute our own paltry petitions for his awesome beneficence.

solitude of March to the growing darkness of December, I felt my arms stretching open wider, wanting to truly see and love in a way I had not before.

Whether dealing with increasingly acrimonious national political discussions or the unknowns of the coronavirus pandemic, we've all been called to make space in our lives for a risky love, a powerful gentleness, that would challenge us to exercise more grace and strength than we thought possible. We're called to give up control, again and again, as new unknowns unfold. But this sort of risky love requires us to demonstrate our own radical hospitality – online and offline – as we reckon with the mystery of the stranger in our midst, the unknown beloved, to whom God has called us to minister.

It may seem odd to refer to the unborn child as "stranger." But that is what he or she is. It is a shock to see the midwife or doctor hold up a freshly birthed baby, red and crying and *real*. For all our intimate knowing of each other, this is our first encounter as separate individuals. For the newborn, the reality of our separation is sensed through vulnerability, cold, and brightness – unpleasant sensations to be hushed and soothed by a mother's arms and breasts. For the mother, however, this meeting is the moment in which we say "hello" to the unique human we've, by some miracle, sustained inside of us, yet now fully see and know as other.

On December 21, a day before my due date, I went into labor. My other two babies arrived late, and so I had suspected I might have a Christmas baby. But my little boy arrived stunningly fast on the winter solstice, letting out his first strong wails only thirty minutes before midnight, as Jupiter and Saturn formed a "double planet" above us. My sweet midwife held up a wailing baby boy, and I stared at him with a shell-shocked grin on my face. Here he was, the unknown beloved I had waited to meet. Since then, he's filled these dark winter days with an indescribable joy.

In *Braiding Sweetgrass*, Robin Wall Kimmerer reminds us that from the first time we hold our newborn children, we realize their growing will all be away from us. But this is what motherhood asks us to do: to hold space, to cultivate a free and open hospitality in which the other is always cherished but never possessed. Kimmerer compares this work to the green algae *Hydrodictyon,* the "water net":

> *Hydrodictyon* is a safe place, a nursery for fish and insects, a shelter from predators, a safety net for the small beings of the pond. . . . But a water net catches nothing, save what cannot be held. Mothering is like that, a net of living threads to lovingly encircle what it cannot possibly hold, what will eventually move through it.

I hold my baby boy knowing that these precious days will pass quickly – into new risks and unknowns, new challenges to love and gentleness. He will not always remain this close, this possessed, cradled safe in my arms. This is the challenge of motherhood: to love wildly, fiercely, determinedly – and then, by God's grace, to let go.

I BELIEVE ONE of our greatest sins is that we are too content. We will take a little of God's life, a little of his goodness, but are often afraid he will give us too much of himself. We are afraid of what the fullness of joy might look like. We don't think we can take it.

And it is true that we can't. There's not enough life in us to match his own, not enough joy in our hearts to comprehend his mirth and delight. We fear God's blessings more often than we ask for them, and seek to substitute our own paltry petitions for his awesome beneficence. We are only willing to go so far, to make so much room. We are afraid of his glorious life, and the risks it might require of us. Like Mary, we must make space: to accept our feebleness and embrace the mystery, knowing that God is good even – and especially – in our weakness and our poverty. As Nouwen says, it is only when we've realized our poverty that we can become good hosts.

"We can only perceive the stranger as an enemy as long as we have something to defend," he writes. "But when we say, 'Please enter – my house is your house, my joy is your joy, my sadness is your sadness and my life is your life,' we have nothing to defend, since we have nothing to lose but all to give."

As I sit here now, cuddling my infant son, I think of the inn where Mary and Joseph were told there was no room. I shudder to think of my own hesitancy and fear as I cracked open the door of my own heart to give this little one room. With my arms filled with the promise I received that quiet Saturday in April, the tears of fear and uncertainty have been replaced with peace, my despair replaced with a quiet, deep joy. There's so much more growing and stretching I have to do. But I am no longer afraid. Welcome, little one. My house is your house, my joy is your joy, my sadness is your sadness, and my life is your life. ➷

EBERHARD ARNOLD

August Macke, *Saint George*, 1912

BEYOND

PACIFISM

SEVEN THESES
ON CHRISTIAN
NONVIOLENCE

Can it ever be a Christian's duty to kill? For Eberhard Arnold, writing in Germany between 1920 and 1935, this question goes to the core of the meaning of Christianity, and of human life.

In the name of Jesus, no one can shed human blood.

In the name of Jesus Christ we can die, but not kill. This is where the gospel leads us. If we really want to follow Christ, we must live as he lived and died.

Speaking to those advocating class war leading to state communism: Again and again in the life of a nation, and in the class struggle for existence, pent-up tensions and conflicts erupt in violent outbursts. These outbursts reveal exploitation and oppression and the savage instincts of covetous passion. People respond in different ways to this violence: some try to uphold law and order by murderous means, while others feel called to fight for social justice with the oppressed.

As Christians, however, we must look further ahead. Christ witnessed to life, to the unfolding of love, to the unity of all members in one body. He revealed to us the heart of his father, who lets his sun shine on the wicked as well as the good. He commissioned us to serve life and to build it up, not to tear it down or destroy it.

Eberhard Arnold (1883–1935) was the founding editor of Plough *and co-founder of the Bruderhof.*

Thus we believe in a future of love and constructive fellowship – in the peace of God's kingdom. And our faith in this kingdom is much more than any wishful longing for the future. Rather, it is a firm belief that God will give us his heart and Spirit now, on this earth. As the hidden, living seed of the future, the church has been entrusted with the Spirit of this coming kingdom. Her present character must therefore show now the same peace and joy and justice that she will embody in the future.

For this reason, we must speak up in protest against every instance of bloodshed and violence, no matter what its origin. Our witness and will for peace, for love at any cost, even our own lives, has never been more necessary. Those who tell us that the questions of nonviolence and conscientious objection are no longer relevant are wrong. Just now, these questions are more relevant than ever. But answering them requires courage and perseverance in love. Jesus knew he would never conquer the spirit of the world with violence, but only by love. This is why he overcame the temptation to seize power over the kingdoms of the earth, and why he speaks of those who are strong in love – the peacemakers – as those who will inherit the land and possess the earth. This attitude was represented and proclaimed strongly by the first Christians, who felt that war and the military profession were irreconcilable with their calling. It is regrettable that serious-minded Christians today do not have the same clear witness.

We acknowledge the existence of evil and sin, but we know it will not triumph. We believe in God and the rebirth of humankind. And our faith is not faith in progress, in the inevitable ascent to greater perfection, but faith in the Spirit of Christ – faith in the rebirth of individuals and in the fellowship of the church. This faith sees war and revolution as necessary judgment on a depraved and degenerate world. Faith expects everything from God, and it does not shy away from the collision of spiritual forces. Rather, it longs for confrontation, because the end must come – and after it, a completely new world.

No one who has heard the clear call of Jesus' Spirit can resort to violence for protection. Jesus abandoned every privilege and every defense. He took the lowliest path. And that is his challenge to us: to follow him on the same way that he went, never departing from it either to the left or to the right (1 Pet. 2:21–23). Do you really think you can go a different way from Jesus on such decisive points as property and violence and yet claim to be his disciple?

Thus there can be no Christian state.

The sword of the Holy Spirit given to the church is totally different in every respect from the sword of governmental authority. God gave the temporal sword, the sword of his wrath, into the hands of unbelievers. The church must make no use of it. The church must be ruled by the one Spirit of Christ alone. God withdrew his Holy Spirit from the unbelievers because they would not obey him. Instead, he gave them the sword of wrath, that is, temporal government with its military power. But Christ himself is the king of the Spirit, whose servants cannot wield any sword but that of the Spirit.

Still, we cannot go to a police officer or a soldier and say, "Lay down your weapons right now, and go the way of love and discipleship of Christ." We have no right to do that. We can do it only when the Spirit speaks a living word to our hearts: "The decisive moment has come for this man to be told." Then we will speak to him, and at the same moment God will tell him. What we tell him must agree with what God says in his heart at the same time.

In the time of the Reformation in the early sixteenth century, our brothers [the first Anabaptists] protested by the thousands against all bloodshed. This powerful movement of the brothers was decidedly realistic. For they never believed that world peace, a universal springtime, was imminent. On the contrary, they believed that the day of judgment was at hand. They expected that the Peasants' War would be a mighty warning from God to the government.

To be aware that the world will always use the sword is realistic. But that realism must be combined with the certainty that Jesus stands free of all bloodshed; he can never be an executioner. He who is executed on the cross can never execute anyone. He whose body is pierced can never pierce or wreck bodies. He never kills; he himself is killed. He never crucifies; he himself is crucified. The brothers say that Jesus' love is the love of the executed one for his murderers, the one who himself can never be a murderer or executioner.

No government can exist without using force. It is impossible to imagine a state that does not use police or military force. In short, there is no government that does not kill. There is no government that does not compromise with capitalism, mammonism, and injustice.

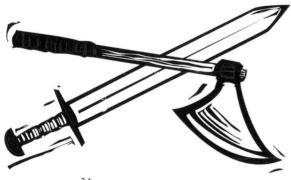

When Jesus said, "Give to Caesar what is Caesar's," he was talking about money (Luke 20:25). He called money something alien, something he had nothing to do with. Give this alien stuff to the emperor; they belong together, mammon and Caesar. Let the money go where it belongs, but give to God what belongs to God. That is what these words mean. Your soul and your body belong not to Caesar but to God and the church. Let your mammon go to the emperor. Your life belongs to God!

Jesus means us to recognize the state as a proven practical necessity. But there can be no Christian state. Force has to rule where love does not.

Pacifism is a misleading caricature of peacemaking.

Nowhere does Jesus say a single word to support pacifism for the sake of its usefulness or benefits. In Jesus we find the deepest reason for living in total nonviolence, for never injuring or harming our fellow human beings, body or soul. Where does this deep inner direction he gives us come from? It has its roots in the deepest source that we sense in one another: the brother or sister in every human being, something of the inner light of truth, the inner light of God and his Spirit (1 John 2:10).

Much good is being said and done in the cause of peace and for the uniting

of nations. But I don't think it is enough. If people feel urged to try to prevent or postpone another major European war, we can only rejoice. But what seems

Nowhere does Jesus say a single word to support pacifism for the sake of its usefulness or benefits.

doubtful is whether they will have much success in opposing the war spirit that exists right now:

When over a thousand of our German people have been killed by Hitler – without a trial – isn't that war? When hundreds of thousands of people in concentration camps are robbed of their freedom and stripped of all dignity, isn't that war? When hundreds of thousands are sent to Siberia and freeze to death while felling trees, isn't that war? When in China and Russia millions of people starve to death while in Argentina and other countries millions of tons of wheat are stockpiled, isn't that war? When thousands of women prostitute their bodies and ruin their lives for the sake of money, isn't that war? When millions of babies are murdered by abortion each year, isn't that war? When people are forced to work like slaves because they cannot otherwise feed their children, isn't that war? When the wealthy live in villas surrounded by parks while other families don't even have a single room to themselves, isn't that war? When some people build up enormous bank accounts while others earn scarcely enough for basic necessities, isn't that war?

We do not represent the pacifism that believes it can prevent future war. This claim is not valid; there is war right up to the present day. We do not advocate the pacifism that believes in the elimination of war through the restraining influence of certain superior nations. We do not support the armed forces of the League of Nations, which are supposed to keep unruly nations in check. We do not agree with a pacifism that ignores the root causes of war – property and capitalism – and tries to bring about peace in the midst of social injustice. We have no faith in the pacifism held by businessmen who beat down their competitors, nor do we believe in the pacifism of people who cannot even live in peace with their own wives. Since there are so many kinds of pacifism we cannot believe in, we would rather not use the word pacifism at all.

But we are friends of peace, and we want to help bring about peace. Jesus said, "Blessed are the peacemakers!" And if we really want peace, we must represent it in all areas of life. We cannot injure love in any way or for any reason. So we cannot kill anyone; we cannot harm anyone economically; we cannot take part in a system that establishes lower standards of living for manual workers than for academics.

We are very much concerned that the objective proclamation of the kingdom of God not degenerate into some new theoretical orthodoxy. We take a lively interest in the socialist and pacifist movements of our day, and we affirm the global conscience they represent – without resorting to their false methods. What we share with them is simply the view that the community of the future will be a life in which all goods are shared freely and lovingly.

IV

Christ calls us to a life of action, not passivity.

The very ordinary demand Jesus makes of his church, namely, to maintain an attitude of love and unconditional kindness, is subject to all manner of misunderstandings. God's language suffers because of such false translation. One example of this is the ineffectual and passive pacifism of the sort advo-cated by Leo Tolstoy. (Gandhi's situation

is different: in his case, nonviolence combined with passive resistance is a weapon for the liberation of his people; it is a form of power politics.)

Tolstoy rightly starts with Jesus' commands in the Sermon on the Mount, where he tells us not to resist evil, to give our coat when our cloak is taken from us; to give two hour's work when one is asked of us; to reconcile with our enemy while we are still on the way with him. But Tolstoy understands these words to mean that we have simply to give in, meekly submitting without clearing up the facts and without protesting against evil. To him the good means simply yielding to an evil fate, without exercising the freedom of will. Thus he in fact advocates the otherworldly, resigned piety of the established church that elsewhere he so sharply condemns. The attitude he demands is, in effect, utmost passivity, a kind of Buddhism. Although he speaks a lot about Jesus, we have to regard Tolstoy as a sort of sectarian monk.

By contrast, Jesus' commands in the Sermon on the Mount have an active meaning, a positive content, namely, that the nature of God in Christ Jesus and in his coming kingdom is revealed here and now in the church. It follows that we cannot yield to any violent government action. God's reign does not give way to the military strength of the great powers. Even though Jesus is executed, he shows throughout the trial that he protests this execution. He does not surrender passively and weakly to the judicial murder. He says, "I am a king,

and you will see the Son of Man at the right hand of the throne of God. You will have to recognize my rule, you who now commit the outrage of killing me."

Jesus' attitude has nothing to do with weak compliance, yet it fulfills the demands of the Sermon on the Mount. This difference is decisive.

Jesus' attitude has nothing to do with weak compliance, yet it fulfills the demands of the Sermon on the Mount. This difference is decisive.

At the time of Jesus, as today, people were waiting for a new world order. They longed for the kingdom of justice of which the prophets had spoken. Then Jesus came, and he disclosed to them the nature and practical consequences of this justice. He showed them a justice completely different from the moral order of the pious and holy – a living, growing power that conformed to the sacred laws of life. He did not give them commands about conduct, but instead radiated the spirit of the future with his very character. That character was unity.

That is why it is fruitless to take any one command of Jesus out of its context and set it up as a law on its own. It is not possible to take part in God's kingdom without purity of heart, without vigorous work for peace; the change of heart must extend to all areas. It is foolishness to try to follow Christ in only one sphere of life. The Beatitudes cannot be taken apart. They begin and end with the same promise of possessing the kingdom of heaven.

The people of the Beatitudes are the people of love. They live from God's heart and feel at home in him. The Spirit of life has set them free from the law of sin and death; nothing can separate them from the love of God in Jesus. And what is most remarkable and mysterious about them is that they perceive everywhere the seed of God. Where people break down under suffering, where hearts long for the Spirit, they hear his footsteps; where the revolutionary desire for social justice arises, where protest against war and bloodshed rings out, where people are persecuted because of their socialism or pacifism, and where purity of heart and compassion can be found – there they see the approach of God's kingdom and anticipate the bliss to come.

Love your enemies – even Hitler.

Nothing else can be commanded of us than what has also been commanded of us in quieter times: that is perfect love.

To our religious socialist and pacifist friends we have to emphasize: Love your enemies. They label Hitler and Mussolini as devils. I cannot find in the New Testament that Jesus called anyone who opposed him a devil (although he

did call some children of the devil); even of Judas Iscariot it is only said, "He *had* a devil." Our enemies, too, remain our brothers and sisters, and the objects of our love.

Love to the enemy is the true love of Jesus. Jesus says, "Blessed are the peacemakers." If our pacifist friends want to be peacemakers, they have to live in love, even toward their enemies. If they hate them, they might also be capable of killing them: "Anyone who hates his brother is a murderer!" (1 John 3:15).

We are commissioned to represent perfect love, also to our enemies. Here there can be no bound or limit; whoever our enemy may be, it makes no difference to whom we offer our love. We love our enemies and want to love them in the right way, so that they come to peace.

We know that we are surrounded by enemies of the Christian faith. In such times the sacrament of forgiveness is needed more than ever, for the enemy's furious hatred challenges us to meet him with the opposite. Our enemies are the very ones we should love by having faith

and understanding for them, knowing that in spite of their blindness they have a divine spark that needs to be fanned.

Love for our enemies has to be so real that it reaches their hearts. For that is what love does. When that happens, we will find the hidden spark from God in the heart of even the greatest sinner. In this sense we must also forgive our enemies, just as Jesus asked the Father to forgive the soldiers who hung him on the cross, saying, "Father, forgive them, for they do not know what they are doing."

How are we to take up this fight? In the Spirit of the coming kingdom, and in no other way. We must fight this battle in love. The weapon of love is the only one we have. And whether we are confronted with a mounted policeman or someone in the Reich Labor Service, whether we come into contact with a district president, a prince, a party leader, or even with the president of the Reich, it makes no difference. We must love them, and only when we truly love them shall we be able to bring them the witness of truth. That is what we are here for.

VI

The Christian way is a soldier's life.

There are some who misunderstand Jesus utterly and think there was a kind of unmanly softness in him. His own words prove that this is not true; he says that his way will lead us into the hardest battles, not only into desperate inner conflicts but even into physical death. His own death and his whole conduct prove it – the sureness and fearlessness with which he met the powers of murder and lying.

After Jesus was killed, the small band of his disciples in Jerusalem proclaimed that though their leader had been shamefully executed, he was indeed still alive and remained their hope and faith as the bringer of the Kingdom. The present age, they said, was nearing its end; humankind was now faced with the greatest turning point ever in its history,

and Jesus would appear a second time in glory and authority. God's rule over the whole earth would be ensured.

The reality of this message in the primitive church could be seen through the working of powers of the future. People

To the early Christians, the military equipment bestowed by the Spirit was a living reality, and not a mere metaphor.

were transformed. The strength to die inherent in Jesus' sacrifice led them to heroically accept the way of martyrdom, and more, it assured them of victory over demonic powers of wickedness and disease. He who rose to life through the Spirit had a strength that exploded in an utterly new attitude to life: love to brothers and sisters and love to one's

enemy, the divine justice of the coming kingdom. Through this Spirit, property was abolished in the early church. Material possessions were handed over to the ambassadors for the poor of the church. Through the presence and power of the Spirit and through faith in the Messiah, this band of followers became a brotherhood.

In their certainty of victory, Christians gathered for the Lord's Supper perceived the alarmed question of Satan and death, "Who is he that robs us of our power?" They answered, exultantly, "Here is Christ, the crucified!"[1] When Christ's death is proclaimed at this meal it means that his resurrection is given substance and life is transformed. His victorious power is consummated in his suffering and dying, in his rising from death and ascent to the throne, and in his second coming. For what Christ has done he does again and again in his church. His victory is perfected. Terrified, the Devil must give up his own. The dragon with seven heads is slain and the evil venom is destroyed.[2]

The trials of all the Greek heroes cannot match the intensity of this spiritual battle. By becoming one with the Christ triumphant, early Christian life became a soldier's life, sure of victory over the greatest enemy in the bitter struggle with the dark powers of this world. Whenever the believers found unity in their meetings, especially when they celebrated baptism and the Lord's Supper and the "Lovemeal" (*Agape*), the

1. Syriac *Testament of Our Lord Jesus Christ*, 1.28.
2. *Ode of Solomon* 22.

power of Christ's presence was indisputable. Sick bodies were healed, demons driven out, sins forgiven. People were assured of life and resurrection because they were freed from all their burdens and turned away from their past wrongs.

Baptism and the confession of faith that those baptized professed were the "symbol" – the "military oath" – through which more and more soldiers of the Spirit were sworn into service. This "mystery" bound them to the service of Christ and the simplicity of his divine works.

It is probably impossible to visualize how seriously the early Christians took the heroic service of the Spirit. The military equipment bestowed by the Spirit was a living reality, and not a mere metaphor. The two basic principles of army life – the right to military pay and the injunction against economic and political involvement – aptly characterized Jesus' commission to his apostles. He stressed their right as soldiers of Christ to receive provisions for their service (although they remained poor on principle) and commanded them to refrain from all business enterprises and the amassing of wealth and possessions. The rule of faith committed all Christians to the apostolic and prophetic soldiership of the Spirit. Non-Christians were therefore called "civilians" or *pagani,* from which the word "pagan" stems.

Jesus had foretold that the drinking of his cup would mean baptism in this bloodbath. Repeatedly the church gathered around the martyrs as for a Lord's Supper celebrated in blood.

Every time, the repulsive spectacle of execution became the solemn victory of Christ over Satan's rule, the certainty of the Lord's resurrection – that event which guaranteed for all times the rule of the dying victor.

VII

We have only one task in the world: to be the body of Christ.

Only very few people in our time grasp this realism of the early Christians. And it is just in this very realistic sense that the Word, which is Christ, wants to find a body in the Church. Mere words about the future coming of God fade away in people's ears. That is why a living reality is needed. Something must be set up, created, and formed, so that no one can pass it by; this is the embodiment, the corporeality.

"Christ in you" is the first part of this mystery. As Christ was in Mary, so Christ is in us who believe and love. Thus we live in accordance with the future; the character of our conduct is the character of God's future.

The life of Jesus had nothing to do with killing and harming others, it had nothing to do with untruthfulness and

impurity, and it had nothing to do with any influence of mammon or property. Jesus went even further: he smote this hostile power in its home territory. His death shattered every weapon of the enemy. But he did still more. He brought the kingdom of God down to the earth, he roused body and soul from death, he himself rose as the Living One, and through his Spirit he laid the foundation for the final kingdom – a kingdom of complete unity for everything in heaven and on earth. He broke down the barriers between nations, and he created the unity of the body of his church as his second incarnation. This new unity and bodily reality of Jesus lives here on the earth in the human race.

This is not something moralistic or legalistic; it is something very natural and simple. It takes place now, through Christ in the Church, by which the future kingdom takes on a physical form. Just for this reason, the Church must demonstrate perfect peace and perfect justice. This is why it cannot shed blood or tolerate private property, cannot lie or take an oath, cannot tolerate the destruction of bridal purity or of marital faithfulness.

The apostle Paul says we are ambassadors of the kingdom of God (2 Cor. 5:20). And the kingdom of God is not represented by any state of this world, but by the Church. This means that we ought to do nothing at all other than what God himself would do for his kingdom. Just as the British ambassador in Berlin does nothing other than the will of his superiors in London, so we too must do the will of God alone. We are no longer subject to the laws of this world; the grounds of our embassy are inviolable, just as in the residence of an ambassador only the laws of the country he represents are valid.

The will of God is to reconcile and to unite. Thus our task too is to reconcile and to unite. We have no other mission in this world. ⤳

These readings are adapted from writings collected in Eberhard Arnold's books, especially God's Revolution *(Plough, 2020) and* Salt and Light, *(Plough, 2014) as well as from texts accessible at EberhardArnold.com. For complete references, see the digital version of this article at* Plough.com/BeyondPacifism.

August Macke, *Saint George*, 1912, oil on canvas

Militant Peacemaking

Eberhard Arnold and Christian Nonviolence

STANLEY HAUERWAS

Pacifism is unrealistic – unless it's conformed to Christ, writes
"America's best theologian" *(Time)* in introducing *Plough*'s new
edition of Eberhard Arnold's classic *God's Revolution*.

"**P**AIN IS THE PLOW that tears up our hearts to make us open to the truth. If it were not for suffering, we would never recognize our guilt, our godlessness, and the crying injustice of the human condition." This is a searing claim I would prefer not to hear but cannot help but acknowledge to be true. To face truths that you would rather not know puts you in a strange position. It is a position I suspect many readers of Eberhard Arnold's *God's Revolution* will find themselves in.

To begin by announcing that a book may challenge how readers understand themselves and their world may seem a doubtful strategy if you want the book to be widely read. I certainly want people to read this book, particularly those who have never known about Eberhard Arnold (1883–1935). I want him read because he is right about what it means to be a Christian. But first and foremost, I want him read because truth is truth. So I'll highlight here some of Arnold's insights to entice readers to have their hearts transformed.

For many, this will be hard going because Arnold, pacifist though he may be, takes no prisoners. His church has little in common with the accommodated Christianity that is so dominant in our culture. As you read you will find yourself thinking, "I have never seen a church like the one he describes." That, of course, is exactly the point. Arnold is determined to help us see what he is sure is God's church, one we no longer see around us. Arnold helps us see because he can write. His writing burns holes in our souls and gives us fresh eyes to see what it means to follow Jesus.

For at the heart of Arnold's account of who we are is Jesus, the Jew of Palestine, and everything that his cross made possible. It is this Jesus who teaches us the intrinsic relation between mammon and murder. It is this Jesus who gives us a way of life with others that we might rightly call church.

Arnold's account of what it means to be a Christian may seem too radical and unrealistic for many. They may admire his vision but not be ready to learn to live, for example, without

---

Peacemaking Is Political

Interview with Stanley Hauerwas by Charles E. Moore

Plough: Stanley, you're a Christian ethicist – what makes Christian ethics Christian?

Stanley Hauerwas: Jesus.

Yes, Jesus. But which Jesus?

It is the Jesus of the Gospels who makes Christian ethics Christian. Of course, part of the difficulty of contemporary Christian ethics is that it tries to be an ethic for anyone, everyone. That's not only

a mistake but tragic. Jesus didn't espouse some "universal ethic"; if he had, he wouldn't have been crucified. No, what determines our way of negotiating with the world is not some rational ethic but a life based on Jesus' life, death, and resurrection.

So-called universal ethics are actually *someone's* ethics disguised as for *anyone*. When that happens, "Jesus" ends up being what Kierkegaard described as our hobbyhorse. That's why I can't

---

Stanley Hauerwas, professor emeritus of theological ethics and of law at Duke University, is author or editor of more than fifty books. This article is the preface to the 2021 edition of Eberhard Arnold's God's Revolution: Community, Justice, and the Coming Kingdom *(Plough 2021).* Plough.com/GodsRevolution

possessions. But Arnold does not think you can do this on your own. Those seeking to be heroic need not apply. Indeed, Arnold is trying to make everyday faithfulness possible.

We dare not forget, moreover, that the heart of Arnold's understanding of the church is the Holy Spirit. It is often said that the Holy Spirit has been ignored in modern theology. That is certainly not true of Arnold's understanding of how the Spirit makes the church possible. Everything he has to say depends on the work of the Spirit. We would be possessed by our possessions if we were not possessed by the Holy Spirit.

Through baptism and the Eucharist the Spirit draws us into the distinctive way of life that makes possible reconciliation between enemies. Such reconciliation is possible because the church is a community of forgiven sinners. So constituted, the church becomes an alternative to the world. Thus Arnold's wonderful remark: "The only way the world will recognize the mission of Jesus is by the unity of his church."

The unity that the Spirit creates comes from the love manifest in the Father's love of the Son and the Son's love of the Father. The communal reality that this love creates is called the kingdom of God. The language of kingdom makes clear that the witness of the church to the world is fundamentally political. The kingdom is a household that, like any household, requires everyday care. To be a Christian is to learn how to share in a common life.

It may be a simplification, but I think in one of his offhand remarks Arnold comes closest to helping us see what makes us Christians. It is very simple – to be a Christian is to be given something to do. When we are baptized we are made citizens in a polity in which we are given good work to do. This work saves us from preoccupation with ourselves and helps us recognize others. Such recognition is rightly called love.

Arnold does not dismiss entirely understandings of salvation that stress the advocate pacifism or some abstract principle of nonviolence. Whose pacifism? Whose nonviolence?

Yet you believe that nonviolence is not just a distinctive mark of discipleship or following Jesus, but an essential one. Why?
Because God incarnate entered our world in a manger and died on the cross. He refused to save us by coercion. Instead, he redeemed the world on the cross, and by enduring such suffering, he gave us an opportunity to see how we can live in the world without killing those who would kill us. Crucifixion is the central act that makes nonviolence intelligible and so powerful.

Christ's salvation offers us the possibility of being grafted into a whole new way of life that is otherwise not possible. In him a new kind of humanity exists, a life together made possible only because of the cross, the resurrection, and the ascension of Christ. Christ does not make the world itself more peaceable. The cross itself is the world's peace, and our task is to live into it and bear witness to it.

You've consistently argued that nonviolence is not a moral rule or a strict commandment – it lies in something deeper.
Well, I wouldn't mind nonviolence being a strict commandment, but it's actually, and more

importance of the individual's experience, but he has little use for pietistic or sentimental forms of the faith. He acknowledges that personal piety has become quite widespread among Christians as a marker of their relationship with God. He judges that this is not a bad thing as long as "personal religious experience" opens the person to growth that leads to service in and for the world. But he insists that the meaning of Christ's cross cannot be restricted to the individual's subjective experience. When salvation is thought to be an individual experience the Christian obligation to pursue justice can be lost.

Arnold challenges those who assume that the kind of community he describes must withdraw from the world. On the contrary, such a community is constantly sending people out. Those sent out will work for justice, but they will also transform what is meant by justice. In particular, they will challenge the presumption that coercion is the only way to achieve justice in a world

of violence. For those who worship a crucified Savior it is simply a contradiction to think the violence of the world can be used to achieve the good. Arnold rhetorically asks how those who have gone out from a place of peace can act in the world differently than they have in the community from which they came.

Arnold is a pacifist, but his pacifism is the expression of his understanding of the conditions necessary for people to live together peaceably. Arnold argues that such a shared way of life entails a profound critique of capitalism. From Arnold's perspective, capitalism is an economic system that underwrites the necessity of possessions. Any attempt to achieve justice in such a system is doomed to fail to the extent that it leaves in place the presumption that what we have is ours.

If members of the church cannot possess possessions, they must learn to share their lives. A common purse becomes not only possible but also necessary. Because a member of the community

importantly, an invitation to a way of life that is committed to telling the truth. And truth is a necessary condition for being able to live without coercion. The way of nonviolence is a hard, long business. It involves being trained in the virtue of patience. But this is the message of the cross. The cross disarms us from having to make the world turn out right. This makes most of us very uncomfortable, but that's the way God's kingdom works.

So truth wins?

Truth wins. Consequently, we don't have to impose it, or enforce it, or even aid it along. That's why patience is crucial to peacemaking. God is

patient, not wanting anyone to perish. We have to live in light of this truth, with ourselves and with others, and we can rest confident that truth will win. But you have to remember, most of us don't want to know the truth. Give us the lie any day.

Part of facing the truth in one's own life is to see how violent one is and can be.

We're not sure what peace looks like anymore. This is why I hate the language of pacifism because it's understood as *not* something. Pacifism is just too passive a notion. The challenge of truthfulness is to learn how to speak about what peace actually is and why it is absent in our world.

does not have any resources to do with as they please, communal discernment is required to test a member's vocation. Being without possessions makes discussion necessary and no doubt some conflict unavoidable. In an interesting way, Arnold's vision of community is profoundly democratic because the weakest member must be heard.

Arnold's account of church is strikingly original but it would be a mistake to think these ideas are original to him. His understanding of the relationship between church and world is closer to the Anabaptist than to any of the other alternatives that came out of the Reformation. But there is also an unmistakable Catholic sensibility in his understanding of the significance of ecclesial practices. Though he emphasizes the voluntary character of church membership, his account seems a far distance from mainline Protestantism.

If I was pushed to locate the tradition Arnold most nearly represents, I would think his community is best understood as a form of monasticism that includes married people. Monastics have always been at the forefront of God's revolution. It is not surprising, therefore, that Arnold's account of marriage challenges romantic presumptions that currently make marriage so problematic. That Arnold devotes so much attention to marriage and the role of children indicates how important he takes these to be for the formation of Christians.

T HERE IS A REASON WHY some reading Arnold might interpret him as withdrawing from the world. While he does not use the distinction between nature and grace that is so dear to Catholics, nor the classical Lutheran dualism between orders of creation and redemption, his basic dualism is that between church and world. He says Christians must acknowledge that God has given the state the "temporal sword," but that means that functions of the state are not tasks to which Christians are called. The state possesses the sword of wrath, but the church and Christians can make no use of it. The one executed on the

---

What does it mean to side with peace and work for it?

To envision peace you have to think concretely. Dorothy Day feeding soup to the poor is the work of peace. The tiredness in her face is peace. "Peacemaking" sounds like it's always a dramatic event. But peace requires the everyday virtue of courage in a world constituted by cowardice and self-interest. Peacemaking takes the work of a whole people, not just one heroic individual. Dorothy Day depended on Peter Maurin, and the two of them on a movement, on a community. We mustn't think of peace as the exception to violence; it's the other way around.

You warned long ago about how fragmentation and isolation breed violence. Is there anything else exacerbating our sense of unpeace? It seems that misinformation is a significant factor.

As Christians we're not sufficiently truthful with one another, and we fail to acknowledge how some forms of Christianity are idolatrous – for instance, those that identify Christianity with American interests or a political party. That needs to be called out for what it is. We're afraid to do that because we think being a Christian is better than not being one. But bad Christianity is very bad, and we need to be more upfront about that.

Don't we have an obligation to at least try to restrain evil in the world?

The police function of the state has to be there. But our real duty, as Christ's reconcilers, lies in

cross executes no one. The same is true of those who would be his followers.

The disavowal of violence may sound like bad news for those concerned that Christians seek justice for the oppressed, but Arnold's understanding of the church makes that a moot criticism. He is adamant that Christians are to be socially engaged in an effort to create societies that are more just. What that means, however, involves imaginative alternatives drawn from the practices of the church. For example, members of his community have not just sought to do something for those suffering from neglect; they have sought to be with those who suffer so that they might share their suffering. Like the Amish who go to be with those who have experienced some destructive event, so Arnold would have the church send out members who first and foremost are a presence for those in pain.

Arnold calls such work for justice "small work," given the scale of suffering in the world. The work may be small, but it is what we have been given to do. As he puts it, "We believe in a Christianity that does something." What an extraordinary insight – to be a Christian is to be in a community that gives you something to do. We are saved by the small tasks that make the lives of others more livable. Thus Arnold's observation that daily work with others is the quickest way to find out if someone is willing to live in community on the basis of genuine love and faith.

It is not just any work Arnold recommends – it is physical work. We should be ready to spend several hours a day doing physical work with our hands. Having started out as a bricklayer myself, I have some appreciation for what Arnold is recommending. Those who work with their hands are drawn out of their self-preoccupations, making it possible to see their neighbor. A neighbor who may turn out to be Jesus in disguise.

I hope I have enticed you to read this book. It is a beautiful book, and beauty may at times wound us. But if we are thus wounded it can be, as Arnold helps us see, what God has given us to save us. ⇒

---

finding ways to live so that the police do not have to carry guns. That's a political position.

So nonviolence is political.
Healthy politics itself can be a form of nonviolence to the extent that I have to listen to what my opponent has to say and not kill him, though I might want to. Nonviolence is more than an attitude. It calls for political engagement in a way that is quite surprising.

Many Christians are wringing their hands over the loss of God in society and of our Christian heritage.
Well, I actually think that one of the good things that is happening today is precisely the loss as Christians of our status and power in the wider society. That loss makes us free. We as Christ's disciples ain't got nothing to lose anymore. That's a great advantage because as a people with nothing to lose, we might as well go ahead and live the way Jesus wants us to. We don't have to be in control or be tempted to use the means of control. We can once again, like the first Christians, be known as that people that don't bullshit the world. Despair is a sin, and I'm hopeful because being a people of peace is ultimately about God's victory in the world. It's not about us. ⇒

This article is excerpted from a longer interview from December 10, 2020. Read the full interview at Plough.com/HauerwasPeacemaking.

Did You Kill Anyone?

Questions They Ask Veterans
Coming Home from War

SCOTT BEAUCHAMP

I KNEW THERE WOULD BE QUESTIONS AFTER THE WAR.

"Did you kill anyone?"

I was ready for that one, the biggest and most intimidating.

That question would hang as an ominous backdrop to nearly every conversation about my time in Iraq, especially prominent in the ones in which I could sense the subject being meticulously avoided. I anticipated the question because it was always there no matter what we were actually talking about.

How I answered depended on who was asking and how the question was put to me. An informal decision tree, intuitive and complex, coalesced in my mind. If the kid asking was bleary-eyed and smiling, swaying drunk on a porch outside of a party, I would demur.

"Oh, don't worry about it, man. I'm just trying to enjoy the party."

Never be eager to indulge the fantasies of young civilians hungry for the illusion of secondhand honor. They don't actually gain anything and you feel vulgar afterwards. Save the vulgarity for the brothers you served with where, rooted in shared experience, gallows humor reaffirms and exalts your bond.

"We don't have to talk about it if you don't want to, but did you kill anyone?"

The question might come from someone who feels obligated to help guide you through your experiences. Their intentions are most likely only superficially magnanimous. They have no idea what they're talking about. Therapy offered so casually is just as presumptuous and shallow as trying to force the personal experience of combat into drunken party conversation.

"I don't think I'm ready to talk about that yet . . ."

The only kind of warrior that people offering therapy understand is a wounded one. You can throw them off of your trail by doubling down on the identity they've assigned you. Their assumptions can become your escape hatch.

Then there are the logistical questions.

"Where were you stationed?"

Germany. But I actually ended up spending more time in Iraq.

"Did you actually . . . you know, kick down doors and stuff?"

Yes. I was in the infantry.

"How long were you in the Army?"

Almost five years. I signed up for four but was stop-lossed.

The logistical questions were easy to answer. Anyone from the Midwest understands that our conversations are built on small talk, and the best small talk is predicated upon logistical data. How long was the flight? Where did you buy that shirt? For how much? It rained two days ago. No, I'm mistaken. It rained three days ago. How old is your son? How many kids? I'm not asking if you're hungry, I'm wondering how long ago you last ate. We're eating in two hours. Not only is small talk polite, but it makes language into a comfortable and familiar meeting place where facts beget facts and everyone has equal access to the common denominator of experience. It has a socially leveling effect. I don't want you to lord your opinions of obscure authors or arcane music over me, I just want to know if you prefer a hard or soft pillow. Because the world we inhabit together, the parts that

Scott Beauchamp is a writer and military veteran whose work has appeared in Paris Review, Atlantic, *and* New York Magazine, *among other places. This article is adapted from his new book,* Did You Kill Anyone?: Reunderstanding My Military Experience as a Critique of Modern Culture *(Zero Books).*

we hold in common, are composed of the mundane. And so if Midwestern Logistical Small Talk seems humble, it also cleverly hides a secret idealistic heart that presumes all of us, everyone, has a world to share. It's a pragmatic type of communion.

I landed in Brooklyn after the war, where Midwestern Logistical Small Talk was mistaken for stupidity. In his essay "What Was the Hipster?," Mark Greif describes the common social denominator that bound together the superficially diverse traits of the last youth movement (if a shift in stylistic emphasis even deserves to be called a movement) as a desultory knowingness rooted in consumerism. In a complicated labyrinth of sophisticated consumer desires, taste is a substitute for wisdom. Taste – with all of its moral weightlessness and novel detachment – can't actually have much significance outside of a six-story walkup.

It can only exist stranded on islands in Brooklyn and Silver Lake and Austin. Shipwrecked from tradition and denuded of intimacy with the larger culture it feeds off of. However sophisticated it might be or however eloquently it's expressed, it has to exist within a narrow matrix of familiar cultural references. Sun Ra. Alan Partridge. Zizek. The Hairpin. Zadie Smith. Walter Benjamin. Tin Tin. Kraftwerk. The same books in the same neat artistic stacks on the same IKEA shelves. The same music echoing through the same sleek minimalist apartments, quarter-filled with the same mid-century modern furniture. And all this isn't to say that a mind-numbing conformity doesn't exist among other American people in other American places, but that a tribe which coalesces around the glib spirit of intellectual novelty, desperate for an empty individuation, inevitably becomes spiritually

David Modell, *John*, from the series "Battle Scarred," exploring the hidden costs of the wars in Iraq and Afghanistan for British soldiers.

Previous spread: David Modell, *Martin*, from the "Battle Scarred" portrait series

David Modell, *Julian*, from the "Battle Scarred" portrait series

anemic. Worse, those in it begin to see their spiritual suffering as a strange sort of victory.

It was a much more dramatic change for me to go from the Army to Brooklyn than it was to go from Missouri to the Army. The total difference can be summed up in the one question I was only asked in Brooklyn and nowhere else. For me, this question became a synecdoche representing the vast space between American cultures.

Why did you join the Army?

It was half meant as an accusation.

Why did you join the Army?

It's not something people do. I remember one particularly confusing conversation where the person I was talking to almost literally couldn't hear what I was saying:

Why did you join the Army if you're an aspiring writer?

It seemed like a better thing to do than going to the University of Iowa.

A long blank stare.

You went to Iowa?

. . . No . . . I joined the Army.

It's not something to do. Who does it? The Eastern Seaboard has one of the lowest rates of enlistment in the country. Imagine what the rate must be among graduates of liberal-arts colleges living in Brooklyn. It's nearly incomprehensible that someone would enlist in the Army.

Why did you join the Army?

I signaled as if I was in their tribe. I watched *Solaris* and even read *Roadside Picnic*. I had a subscription to the *New York Review of Books* and maybe I would mention Robert Duncan's *The H. D. Book* during brunch. These points of reference were constellations used to navigate social waters that were actually never too far from familiar shores for the Brooklyn tribe. The variation within them, whether you prefer this writer over that, was all just the narcissism of small differences. The point was that by even having an opinion existing between a stable orthodoxy of cultural bookends, you were expressing a fundamental commonality. You act like one of us, but we don't join the Army. So why did you?

Why did you join the Army?

It makes sense in the tribe to go to grad school. To spend most of the waking hours of the rest of your life in a classroom. To volunteer overseas for a secular NGO. To not work at all and spend your parents' money instead. To retire when you're twenty-five. To write and publish your memoirs when you're nineteen. To be too busy meditating and skateboarding to work. To be too busy working at a bookstore to meditate or skateboard. To professionally promote parties. To take workshops about how to grow up. To do anything other than serve in the military.

Why did I join the Army? I didn't know how to answer the question. At least not the way they were asking it in Brooklyn. Of course, I'd been asked before. I'd even been asked by other soldiers while I was in the Army, but then the question had been posed with shades of Midwestern Logistical Small Talk. Here was no critical arrow piercing the heart of the action itself. The question didn't come from some fundamental misunderstanding. They weren't asking why anyone would join the Army at all, but what particular set of circumstances led me to join. More than anything else, it was a way to get to know about someone's life before the Army.

Why did you join up?

My father and grandfather and his father before him all served.

My kids needed healthcare.

I wanted money for college.

My uncle wants me to be a police officer like him and he said this is the best way to go about it.

Underneath each of these answers was a basic agreement (usually) about the honor of the venture. No one joins the military just for money or solely out of love of family. It's too profound and uniquely complex a sacrifice for that. And when a young person tells you he enlisted for adventure, what he really means is that he went on a quest for meaning – our popular vocabulary being too anemic to support the weight of a desire simultaneously so necessary and recondite. We don't have the words to describe our hunger. We struggle to articulate both the depth of our appetite and what might be required to sate it. And there are a lot of reasons why people join up. Some are unutterable. And of those that we can express, many contradict each other. When it comes to something like swearing loyalty to a warring army during a time of combat, motivations can't necessarily be seen through a Manichean lens.

So I tried to think of the question the Brooklynites should have asked if they really wanted to understand something so alien to them. A question that doesn't emit vague antagonism, but one that could possibly draw us closer together and that we could both learn from. Something that would help us understand each other. One day the question posed itself to me.

Do you miss it?

> **You act like one of us, but we don't join the Army. So why did you?**

Behind the Black Umbrellas

Debating Violence With Portland's Antifa

PATRICK TOMASSI

"**W**HAT'D YOU SEE?" a man shouted. Around him, a crowd of black-clad activists gathered outside the Multnomah County Democrats building in northeast Portland, Oregon, the Sunday night after the US presidential election in November 2020.

"You didn't see shit!" the protesters chanted in response. Several people with hammers, rocks, and cans of spray paint broke windows of the building and tagged it – "Fuck Biden," "ACAB," "BLM." Others opened black umbrellas, shielding the vandals from security cameras and passersby. The chanting continued: "Whose lives matter? Black Lives Matter!" and "All Cops Are Bastards" (to the tune of "nana nana boo boo"). Two men with drums kept rhythm for the chants. Within minutes, most of the windows were broken and the group was on the move again, back through neighborhood streets towards Laurelhurst Park.

> ## "If there's a Nazi, they should probably be punched."
>
> *Buckets*

During summer 2020, as my hometown was front and center in the national news, I found that my idea, and other Portlanders', about exactly what was going on was largely determined by what media we relied on: conservatives and liberals seemed to be living in alternate universes, with the same timelines but different facts. After one more argument about whether downtown Portland was actually "on fire," I decided to begin attending and reporting on the nightly demonstrations.

When I arrived at Laurelhurst Park earlier that November evening, first-aid volunteer Marie Tyvoll had just finished setting up a medical tent. She introduced me to some other activists; most saw my press badge and faded into the shadows. None were willing to talk to me. Some said I should leave. After about half an hour, I overheard a man talking about his desire to "punch a Nazi." The man ("Buckets," for his plastic drum) wore the full "black bloc," head-to-toe black including a balaclava, and looked to be in his twenties or thirties. He told me that for him it was pretty simple. "If there's a Nazi, they should probably be punched." Who qualified as a Nazi? Not run-of-the-mill Trump supporters. But Proud Boys? Probably. He said that it was "highly likely" that he had been at events where Proud Boys had also been present, but refused to answer when I asked if he had ever punched a Nazi, although he said he had been punched by one.

While Buckets and I were speaking, another activist addressed the crowd. I raised my camera to take a photograph. "Hey, no filming," yelled a large man in a gas mask. The fact that I was taking stills didn't count: "No pictures means no pictures. Get the fuck out," he said, towering over me. I hesitated for a moment. "We're not gonna ask you again. Get the fuck out." I walked away; he followed me briefly. The speaker asked the crowd how many were excited about Joe Biden, and was answered with boos. He proposed that they go "have some fun" at Democratic headquarters. Someone in the crowd started a chant: "ADAB – All Democrats Are Bastards!" It was hard to fit to the "nana nana" melody, and didn't catch on.

When the group began marching through Laurelhurst about 10 p.m., Buckets and another man drummed a rhythm for the chants. As they marched, activists shone flashlights into residents' windows. Some residents stepped out on their porches. Others peeked out from behind closed blinds. Marchers pulled election

---

Patrick Tomassi is a teacher and writer in Portland, Oregon, his native city. He helps organize the annual New York Encounter and is a contributing editor at Veritas Journal.

signs from people's lawns and tossed them into the street. One was for Mingus Mapps, the Black candidate who had unseated City Commissioner Chloe Eudaly earlier that week. Eudaly had been highly supportive of the protests. Mapps had received an endorsement from the Portland Police Union.

The direct action at the Democrats' building lasted less than ten minutes. The police were nowhere in sight. But as the group began to wind back toward the park, a number of officers arrived on bicycles. They followed for several blocks, then closed in at the middle of an intersection, arresting three men. Activists yelled at the police, asking why the men were being arrested. A moment later a man shouted, "Everyone scatter – let's go!" "Be water," said others, and the group dissolved into side streets.

The Fascist Next Door

A quite different "direct action" took place on January 6, 2021, in Washington, DC, when an angry mob of Trump supporters stormed the US Capitol. Among them were Proud Boys including organizer Joe Biggs; believers in the QAnon conspiracy theory including Jacob Chansley, better known as the QAnon Shaman; and known White nationalists and neo-Nazis including livestreamer Tim Gionet, known as "Baked Alaska." They roamed the building, trying to find Vice President Pence and the legislators who had moments earlier been attempting to certify the electoral college results; court filings disagree about what they would have done had they found them. Ultimately five people died in the insurrection.

For many Americans, the Capitol insurrection came as a shock. For anti-fascist activists, it was exactly what they had expected. For years they have been saying that far-right violence, including terrorist attacks in which people are killed, is on the rise both in the United States and globally.

The evidence bears this out. In October 2020, months before the Capitol attack, the Department of Homeland Security published

Marie Tyvoll, a first-aid volunteer, confronts Portland police, July 2020.

Previous spread: Protesters take cover during an assault on the Portland federal courthouse, July 2020.

Photograph by Spencer Platt/Getty Images

Proud Boys rally in Portland, September 2020

a "Homeland Threat Assessment" investigating terrorist attacks and killings committed by "domestic violent extremists." The report notes that "2019 was the most lethal year for domestic violent extremism in the United States since the Oklahoma City bombing in 1995." Among domestic violent extremists, the report notes, White supremacists committed eight of the total sixteen lethal attacks, and were responsible for thirty-nine of the forty-eight resulting deaths. Elsewhere the report predicts that "racially and ethnically motivated violent extremists – specifically white supremacist extremists (WSEs) – will remain the most persistent and lethal threat in the Homeland" in the coming years. (The document also discusses militant anarchists as a potential threat.)

A similar tone is struck in the lengthy "Country Report on Terrorism" published in 2019 by the US State Department. "The threat posed by racially or ethnically motivated terrorism (REMT), particularly white supremacist terrorism, remained a serious challenge for the global community," it states. "Continuing a trend that began in 2015, there were numerous deadly REMT attacks around the world in 2019, including in Christchurch, New Zealand; Halle, Germany; and El Paso, Texas."

According to the nonpartisan Center for Strategic and International Studies, right-wing extremist groups kill vastly more people than do left-wing ones. "Between 1994 and 2020, there were 893 terrorist attacks and plots in the United States. Overall, right-wing terrorists perpetrated the majority – 57 percent – of all attacks and plots during this period, compared to 25 percent committed by left-wing terrorists, 15 percent by religious terrorists, 3 percent by ethnonationalists, and 0.7 percent by terrorists with other motives." In the United States in the years since 9/11, "right-wing terrorist attacks caused 335 deaths, left-wing attacks caused 22 deaths, and ethnonationalist terrorists caused 5 deaths."

A real rise in right-wing extremist violence, then, long predates January 6, 2021. And antifa groups have come to see themselves as the ones willing to stand up and fight Hitler before he comes to power.

Anti-Fascist Origins

Over the summer of 2020, anti-fascist activists in Portland were catapulted into the national spotlight by their participation in racial-justice protests, street fights with far-right groups and law enforcement, and vandalism. In September, President Trump called Portland an "anarchist jurisdiction," and the Justice Department soon made a similar designation. But Portland has a long history of anarchist and anti-fascist activity.

Oregon's anti-fascist presence arose as a response to right-wing extremism. Though recently famous for its lefty "Portlandia" reputation, the state has for most of its history been home to significant numbers of far-right and White supremacist groups. In 1859, it became the only state admitted to the union with a Black exclusion law. In 1922, Walter Pierce, a Klansman, was elected governor of the state. The Black exclusion law was overturned in 1926, but was not fully removed from the state constitution until 2002.

In November 1988, skinhead neo-Nazis from a group called East Side White Pride beat Ethiopian student Mulugeta Seraw to death with a baseball bat in front of his apartment in southeast Portland. The incident provoked Mic Crenshaw, co-founder of Anti-Racist Action (ARA), to move from Minneapolis to Portland to found an ARA chapter there. This group gave rise in 2007 to Rose City Antifa, the first group in the United States to adopt the "antifa" moniker, which is common in Europe.

Groups like Rose City Antifa subscribe to a set of views often described as anarcho-communism. They use symbols like the three-arrow Iron Front emblem of the German anti-Nazi Social Democratic Party, and the red and black flag emblem representing both communism and anarchism. According to Mark Bray of Rutgers University, the roots of contemporary antifa lie in pre- and immediately post-World War II Europe. In his book *Antifa: The Anti-Fascist Handbook*, Bray tells the story of the "43 Group," a collection of mostly Jewish British veterans who set out to prevent fascists from organizing in England in the years directly following the war. Fascists and nationalists, including former members of the British Union of Fascists, were by this time organizing events under slogans such as "War on the Jews." Because police would not simply shut down fascist groups' events, the 43 Group attempted to force them to, using direct-action techniques. "If a single member could get through the cordon of fascist stewards to tip over the speaker's platform," Bray writes, "the police had a policy of not allowing the fascists to set it up again. With that in mind, the 43 Group organized units of about a dozen into wedge formations that, at an agreed time, would start far out in the crowd and build up steam so that they 'could break through many times [their] number of muscular stewards' and get to the platform." If this didn't work, the group would disperse into the crowd to start fistfights, creating a brawl the police would have to shut down. According to Bray, this approach was hugely successful.

Present-day antifa groups see themselves as belonging to the tradition of the 43 Group and other groups that opposed the rise and resurgence of fascism around Europe. They engage in similar tactics, using direct-action techniques, they say, to defend marginalized communities – particularly ethnic and racial minorities, and queer and trans people – from those who would commit violence against them. "Our long-term goal," one Portland activist told me, "is to make it so that people who are organizing for violence against our communities don't have a platform to do so." They understand violence, in a broad sense, to encompass actions that do harm, whether or not they involve a physical attack. Anti-fascists "doxx" people – publish their personal information in an attempt to affect them financially and socially – though Rose City Antifa claims only to doxx those who have made threats or acts of violence against marginalized people. Others are not so scrupulous – for example, one anti-fascist activist attempted to doxx me, publishing my place of employment and the name of a journal I help edit, after I shared photographs from the Democratic headquarters march in November.

Antifa activists also believe, at least in the United States, that the police and prison systems themselves are fundamentally racist institutions that must be abolished; a common chant at direct-action events is "no good cops in a racist system." Most antifa seek to abolish the state entirely, and establish what Rose City Antifa refers to as "a classless society, free from all forms of oppression." One person I spoke with in August during a direct action near the Portland Police Union building told me that the point is to put stress on the system. "If we've learned anything," he said, "it's to be really annoying. . . . We're putting cracks in the system . . . overtaxing it" to provoke the police into using excessive force. He added that "every single act of aggression that they commit against people that are coming out here . . . just makes our argument stronger as well."

This approach was extremely effective throughout the summer, with fireworks lobbed

> ## "If we've learned anything, it's to be really annoying."
>
> *An antifa activist*

at the police and Molotov cocktails repeatedly thrown at the federal courthouse, starting fire after fire. Tensions escalated: more police and federal law enforcement officers were sent to the city; nightly protests repeatedly ended with police using tear gas and other "less lethal" munitions to disperse the crowd. Protesters captured numerous video clips of excessive force, including the now-iconic one of federal agents attacking a peaceful US Navy veteran.

The Language of the Unheard

"I think a riot is the language of the voiceless," an anti-police activist in Portland told me during a protest on election night, paraphrasing, like many others I spoke to, a 1967 speech by Martin Luther King Jr. "In the final analysis," said King, "a riot is the language of the unheard."

People recall this phrase at critical moments; following the police killings of Michael Brown Jr., Eric Garner, and Tamir Rice, Google searches for it spiked. In April, 2015, during the Baltimore riots following Freddie Gray's death in police custody, it was googled more frequently than King's more well-known observation about light driving out darkness and love driving out hate. After George Floyd's death in 2020, during the sometimes-violent protests that ensued, the quote was searched for four times as often as during the Baltimore riots and used in hundreds of articles, both those critical of rioting and those that sought to explain it.

In a June *New Yorker* article, Keeanga-Yamahtta Taylor used it to condemn ongoing oppression:

> Riots are not only the voice of the unheard . . . they are the rowdy entry of the oppressed into the political realm. They become a stage of political theatre where joy, revulsion, sadness,

anger, and excitement clash wildly in a cathartic dance. They are a festival of the oppressed.

But journalists like Taylor and others did not go on to point out, as King did in his speech, that riots tend to aggravate the very problems they seek to address. Riots are not only the voice of the unheard, King declared; they are also "socially destructive and self-defeating." "I will continue to condemn riots, and continue to say to my brothers and sisters that this is not the way. And continue to affirm that there is another way. But at the same time, it is as necessary for me to be as vigorous in condemning the conditions which cause persons to feel that they must engage in riotous activities as it is for me to condemn riots."

Later in November, I spoke with two representatives from Rose City Antifa. We sat outside at a picnic bench in a park a few blocks from the house where I grew up. The evening was cold, but unusually dry for the time of year. When I arrived at the park, I was surprised to see that the activists, who asked to be called Johnny and Taylor, wore casual street clothes and made no effort to disguise their identities. As they spoke, steam wafted off their KN95 masks, fogging their glasses.

"We support a diversity of tactics," Taylor told me when asked about the vandalism that has made antifa notorious. "I think that a lot of the property destruction we're seeing right now is a product of people's genuine and justified frustration and rage with any number of things in our society." Taylor pointed to a lack of response on the part of politicians to the problem of police brutality, as well as frustration about the quarantine and poor handling of the pandemic. "We don't comment on the actions that people choose to take."

"We try to not comment or speculate on what people's motivations might be," Johnny added, "because we believe that there are no bad protesters. . . . We try to be empathetic to any reason that people would show up to a protest and put themselves out there like that."

"I don't know that there would be a 'right' answer," Taylor interjected. "I can't think of a thing that would sway me either way about why someone would break a window."

Johnny told me that, for Rose City Antifa, self-defense can be "preemptive." It is not necessary to wait until someone is prepared to inflict violence before you defend yourself. Instead, by community organizing, doxxing, and occasionally brawling in the streets, antifa groups believe they can prevent greater violence later.

"We believe that there are no bad protesters."
Johnny

These activists, like most of the others I spoke with, also wanted to broaden the definition of "violence" that I used to frame my questions. "If you think of destruction and violence as things that do harm," Johnny told me, "then we see that in our city all the time. We see that there's a housing crisis in Portland; we see that wages have not been adjusted to allow for everyone in the city to have a good quality of life; there are houses that are sitting empty, accumulating property value while people sleep on the streets. Those are things that are violent." When protesters act out of frustration with this kind of violence, Johnny said, "What's a window to that?"

I told them about a Somali immigrant woman in Minneapolis whose restaurant was destroyed in the first days of the racial-justice protests, and asked Johnny and Taylor how they thought about the unintended consequences of property destruction. They disputed my use of the word "unintended." "People

NO PUBLIC
RESTROOM
PORTLAND LOO
ONE BLOCK WEST

Smiley, who lives on the streets of Portland, was affected when an antifa action shuttered homeless outreach at St. André Bessette church.

pretty much know that things can happen when they engage in this sort of action," Johnny said. "And I think that in its aftermath, our goal is still to keep our communities safe and healthy. The community will try to address those issues."

"People make mistakes," Taylor added. "Things happen in the heat of the moment that people might not have chosen to do otherwise. I think that what matters most is how we as a community bounce back from that and show each other that we take care of each other."

One such "mistake" was made in downtown Portland the night after the election, when a black-bloc activist with a hammer shattered the windows of St. André Bessette Catholic Church. In the security footage, a homeless woman who had been sleeping in the doorway can be seen jumping out of the way in terror. The parish, whose primary work is to provide meals and clothing to Portland's homeless community, was forced to close down operations for two weeks due to safety concerns.

I spoke with the pastor, as well as several of the people who live on the streets in the area and rely on St. André for both support and companionship. They all expressed frustration that someone would choose to harm vulnerable people. "It was terrible. It was selfish. Uncalled for," a man named Smiley told me. "I don't think they care about people on the street."

Rose City Antifa did not step forward to help St. André Bessette rebuild. Those who did were members of the church community, strangers, and at least one formerly homeless person who had been helped by the parish. Nor did any antifa group take responsibility for the attack – a benefit of the decentralized anarchist approach. The man who committed the crime, one is meant to believe, acted alone.

Justifiable Violence?

Most antifa activists I've spoken with do not consider property destruction violence: violence, they say, can only be directed at people. In antifa circles, this sort of violence is often referred to as "punching Nazis," and is a matter of intense debate among leftist and anti-fascist groups. So-called "everyday anti-fascists" tend to be ambivalent about it, while others, like Buckets, are more explicit in their endorsement. Johnny, who grew up in a faith tradition, said that the idea of committing violence in response to injustice had not always been palatable. But this started to change as Johnny began to empathize with those committing the violence. "People generally aren't pushed to violence on a micro-scale" such as face-punching, said Johnny, "unless they have exhausted other resources."

Johnny and Taylor explained that they are willing to punch Nazis for the same reason that they doxx them: to provide real-world consequences for threatening and perpetrating acts of violence. In this sense, it is fundamentally about power. Antifa groups cannot make the people they see as Nazis change, but they can make it so costly to be a Nazi – economically, socially, or physically – that they stop showing up. "If you and your buddies posted that you were going to go commit violence against members of a race of people," Taylor said, "and then you lost your jobs, and had to go spend time looking for new ones," or your friends abandoned you when they learned about your behavior, "you might think twice about doing that." Similarly, if every time you showed up at a Proud Boy rally you got punched, you might get sick of it and stop showing up.

Both activists said that while they'd come to support violence as a political tool they were by no means cavalier about it. "Violence still makes me incredibly sad and incredibly upset," Taylor told me. "For us as an organization," Johnny added, "violence is always a last resort." This was similar to what I heard from people carrying weapons such as baseball bats and truncheons at direct-action events.

Antifa activists – including every one that I spoke with – repeatedly claim that they do not go looking for a fight. "We aren't punching first," Taylor told me. "The work that we do is community self-defense. And we're pretty clear about [the fact] that the Nazis who get punched are people who are coming into our city looking to inflict violence on people who they see as 'other.'"

Activists on the far right completely disagree about who's looking for a fight. When I asked "Bluto," a Proud Boy, at a September rally about the large baseball bat he was leaning on, he corrected me. "My war club," he said. "It is defensive only, and lower body. Because anything above that would definitely do some real damage. I'm willing to defend myself, but I don't want to go to jail for murder, and I don't feel somebody necessarily needs to die."

"I got something to add," another Proud Boy chimed in. "You know how you haven't seen violence happen here? You won't. Not here." Proud Boys, they agreed, do not throw the first punch. Bluto said he would go to the wall for his right to act in self-defense. "But I insist that I will never start a fight."

And yet, as I wrote in *Public Discourse* in November, violence does break out almost any time Proud Boys and antifa interact. These events are powder kegs, waiting for one spark before they blow. Each side blames the other, and says that the bats, pepper-spray canisters, and guns that people on their own side carry are for self-defense only. Video footage, sometimes selectively edited to make the other side appear at fault, is circulated on social

> **"It was terrible. It was selfish. Uncalled for. I don't think they care about people on the street."**
>
> *Smiley*

media and used to radicalize and recruit more militants on both sides.

In *Antifa*, Mark Bray makes a case in defense of violent anti-fascism. While he accepts that confronting far-right groups could give them more attention than they would get otherwise, he claims that it also prevents them from capitalizing on it. He points to the 2017 Berkeley protests, in which militant anti-fascists clashed with far-right extremists and neo-Nazis, threw fireworks and rocks, broke windows, and set fires, in a successful attempt to cancel right-wing speaker Milo Yiannopoulos's event.

> ## "How can you hate me, when you don't even know me?"
> ### *Daryl Davis*

"Yiannopoulos's fame did indeed soar after he was shut down in Berkeley," Bray writes. However, if shutting him down "prevented a single undocumented or transgender student from facing harassment or worse . . . then it was worth it. Period." The event he is discussing is one at which multiple people, including bystanders, were injured.

Bray suggests that, since World War II is "the least controversial war in American history," the question is not really whether Americans think it is legitimate to fight Nazis. Rather, the question is whether Americans would consider it heroic to do so *before* the outbreak of the war. Why, he wonders, do Americans object to the idea of confronting present-day fascists and White supremacists with violence, when they have no such objections to battling Hitler? For Bray, the question of whether an explicitly fascist regime could actually come to power today is irrelevant, because whether or not they are in power, far-right extremists can still inflict harm on marginalized communities.

Another Way to Combat Hate

During summer 2019, I drove for Lyft to make extra money. One day I had a discussion with a young woman who was flying home to visit her family. She talked about the difficulties of coming out as lesbian to her conservative parents, and how hard it had been to talk with them. At some point in the conversation, I brought up the Black blues musician Daryl Davis, who has spent decades befriending men in the Ku Klux Klan. Over the years, hundreds of people have left the hate group as a result. "I used to think dialogue like that was possible," she told me as we pulled up to the airport. "I don't anymore. That's why I participate in anti-fascist actions now." She picked up her luggage and walked inside.

This is a common refrain among those who participate in anti-fascist actions. As one man said of Nazis at a Mark Bray reading, "You are not going to love these people away." "I wasn't planning on it," Bray responded. Taylor and Johnny, of Rose City Antifa, agreed with the woman from my Lyft and the man at the reading. "I don't think that dialogue is possible because dialogue requires good faith on the part of both parties," Johnny said, "and I don't think that that is possible with people who have gone to that far of the right." By the point someone is a neo-Nazi, Johnny said, "a dialogue ship has sailed."

Just before Christmas, I spoke with Daryl Davis over Zoom from his home in Maryland. Davis has spent the last thirty-seven years engaging with members of hate groups, including Klansmen and neo-Nazis. Growing up, he said, he would have agreed that the ship had sailed. When he was ten years old, Davis, who is Black, was carrying the flag during a march with his otherwise all-White Cub Scout troop when spectators began throwing

rocks and bottles at him. That was when he first started to ponder the question that would end up shaping much of his life: "How can you hate me," he wondered, "when you don't even know me?" He began to read books about racists and hate groups, but none could answer his question.

In 1983, Davis was playing with a country band at a truck-stop bar called the Silver Dollar Lounge in Frederick, Maryland, fifty miles west of Baltimore, when a White man walked up to him during a break in the show. He put his arm around Davis and told him he was the only Black man he'd ever heard play the piano like Jerry Lee Lewis. "Where do you think Jerry Lee Lewis learned how to play?" Davis asked. When Davis said that Lewis learned his style from Black blues and boogie-woogie players, the man did not believe him. He was fascinated by Davis, though, and invited him to his table for a drink, the first time, he said, he'd ever had a drink with a Black man. In their ensuing conversation, the man said that

he was a member of the Ku Klux Klan. Davis didn't believe him, he told me, until the man showed him his membership card. At the end of the conversation, the man gave Davis his phone number and told him to call whenever the band was in town. He did, and the man came every time, sometimes bringing other Klan members along to see the Black man who played like Jerry Lee.

In 1987 or '88, it occurred to Davis that the answer to the question that had plagued him since childhood – *how can you hate me, when you don't even know me?* – had fallen into his lap. "Who better to ask that question of," Davis thought, "than somebody who would join an organization that practices that kind of thing?" He got back in contact with the man from the Silver Dollar Lounge and asked him to put him in touch with the Klan leader for the state of Maryland. Then Davis traveled around the United States, meeting with members of the Klan to find the answer to his question. "I never set out to convert any of them," Davis said. He

Proud Boys and Patriot Prayer demonstrators in Portland, September 2020

had been raised to know that a tiger cannot change its stripes. But within a few years, people started leaving the Klan because of him.

"I never expected some Klan leader I'm talking to to decide to quit based on some of the things that I've been saying to him," Davis told me. "He quit. I got his robe and hood. It was a shock to me." Davis said that, like the woman in my Lyft, his thinking had been wrong. "She was thinking like I was . . . The thing of it is, that's right. A tiger

Daryl Davis

cannot change its stripes and a leopard cannot change its spots, because they were born with those stripes and spots. A Klansman or White supremacist is not born with that robe and hood." Davis now has over fifty sets of robes and hoods, and more than two hundred men have left racist hate groups either directly because of him, or because of someone he helped.

Davis said that the mistake anti-fascist activists make is to try to deny someone's reality. "Whatever somebody perceives becomes their reality," he said. "Whether it's real or not, it's their reality because that's what they perceive." He used the example of crime statistics. "They see more Black people in prison than White people. And that's a fact: there are more Blacks in prison than White people. So their perception is Black people are more prone to crime than White people." But they are not looking at all the data, from poverty to educational differences to imbalance in the justice system. Instead of yelling at them that they are wrong, Davis tries to fill out the picture. "I offer them different things to look at. And then they

put it together themselves. And that is a lot stronger than trying to compel somebody's behavior. When you try to force somebody to do something, you're going to have resistance. You might get them to do it, but it's going to be short-lived. But if they come into it themselves, it's going to last a lot longer." For Davis, this is no armchair philosophy. He has had guns pulled on him, and stood next to fiery crosses. He has seen conversion happen hundreds of times, and many of the men who have left violent hate groups because of their friendships with him have gone on to help others leave.

In 2019 Daryl Davis was invited to speak at an event on racism and free speech organized by a media platform called Minds. After anti-fascist activists allegedly threatened to blow up the event, it was moved from New Jersey to a secret location in Philadelphia. Somehow, Davis said, activists got wind that the after-party would be taking place back in New Jersey. They showed up across the street to protest. According to Davis, they were calling those inside White supremacists. So he decided to invite them in so they could meet everyone. "So I invited them over, and they called me a White supremacist. I mean, when you call me a White supremacist, that battle is over, you know? It was done."

Davis said that he is sympathetic to anti-fascist activists who are concerned about White supremacy. "They want to punch a Nazi in the face," he said. "I get it, but you know, that does not work. I know a lot of Nazis. I know a lot of Klansmen. And while I don't agree with their views, I can tell you one thing: I've never seen anybody punch the Nazi out of a Nazi. It doesn't work. All it does is empower them, enable them." He said that fighting always escalates. Fists are traded for guns. "You put a bullet in somebody, they don't come back."

ANDREA GROSSO CIPONTE

FREIHEIT!

THE WHITE ROSE GRAPHIC NOVEL

(AN EXCERPT)

UNIVERSITY OF MUNICH, FEBRUARY 18, 1943

> Every people deserves the regime it is willing to endure.

> But now the end is at hand.

Andrea Grosso Ciponte is a painter, graphic novelist, filmmaker, and illustrator who teaches at the Academy of Fine Arts in Catanzaro, Italy. He is the author of Renegade: Martin Luther, The Graphic Biography *(Plough, 2017) and* Freiheit!: The White Rose Graphic Novel *(Plough, 2021). Learn more about* Freiheit! *at* Plough.com/Freiheit.

FEBRUARY 22, 12:45 P.M.

Sophie Scholl, Hans Scholl, and Christoph Probst were the first three members of the White Rose to be executed, on February 22, 1943. The execution report recorded Hans Scholl's last words: "Long live freedom."

A Life That Answers War

The Story of Conscientious Objection and the Bruderhof

SCOTT BUTTON

WHEN I WAS SIX, our family moved within walking distance of my grandparents, and I loved visiting them several evenings a week. I would spend the time playing checkers with Opa, my grandfather, while Oma busied herself making us a plate of food: usually some slices of the hard, fermented German sausage that always hung on the sideboard, with a cup of maté, a South American tea, for Opa. The melding of cultures seemed normal to me, as was Opa and Oma's lapsing into Spanish or German when they wanted to speak privately. As I grew, we moved on to chess, then various card games,

Conscientious objectors perform "work of national importance" during World War II in a Civilian Public Service camp, Waldport, Oregon.

Scott Button, a member of the Bruderhof, lives in Rifton, New York, with his wife and two children. He serves as the Bruderhof's associate general counsel.

and ultimately settled on conversation. Opa didn't like to talk about himself, and even less about his past, but when the stories did come out they were captivating. Over time I began to piece together the route by which he'd acquired such diverse cultural tastes. I learned how the twists and turns along the way had been driven, in large part, by a committed opposition to violence in all forms. Opa was an ardent conscientious objector himself. But resistance to war had shaped his life from the cradle.

Jakob Gneiting was born in Germany in 1933, at the Bruderhof, a Christian intentional community on a farm in the Rhön Mountains. His father, Alfred, had grown up in a socialist family. Despite finding the established churches too dismissive of social inequities, Alfred felt drawn to Christianity. In 1924, a friend encouraged him to visit the Bruderhof community, founded four years earlier with the goal of living out the practical implications of Jesus' Sermon on the Mount. Alfred was inspired by the community's vision, but wasn't ready to commit himself. Following several years of coming and going and the patient conversation of Bruderhof founder Eberhard Arnold, Alfred finally decided to join. Shortly thereafter, Gretel Knott answered a newspaper advertisement for employment at the community, which needed a kindergarten teacher. Also inspired by the Bruderhof's witness, she joined within a few years. Alfred and Gretel were married in 1931. Jakob was the first of their seven children.

From its inception, the Bruderhof had been committed to conscientious objection to all participation in violence and war.[1]

> **Resistance to war shaped my grandfather from the cradle.**

The Bruderhof took part in many of the peace conferences that were held under the auspices of the International Fellowship of Reconciliation. Over time, members sought out connections with others holding the same convictions: Quakers in Britain, Dutch Mennonites, Dietrich Bonhoeffer.[2] Eberhard Arnold had studied the first Anabaptists, and the pacifism and communitarianism of the sixteenth-century Hutterites in the Tirol had a particular influence on the Bruderhof. Like these original Anabaptists, the Bruderhof found themselves in a Europe repeatedly convulsed by war.

By 1933, the Bruderhof and the Third Reich were already squaring off in opposition. Nevertheless, the Bruderhof pressed on in its vision of demonstrating the nature of God's coming kingdom. Late that year, community members wrote to various government officials requesting accommodation of their pacifist position. To Reich President Paul von Hindenburg, they wrote, "Our brotherhood requests that it may serve the German Reich and its government in works of love as a traditional German Christian community in the way that the Hutterian Brethren have done faithfully for four hundred years, without taking part in military, political, or judicial actions." Members of the community had all participated in drafting the letter. "What makes me especially happy," Alfred said about the text, "is that the two tasks have been differentiated so clearly: the task of the church and the task of the state. It is a powerful witness."[3]

Pacifist Refugees

As the Nazi party consolidated power in Germany, the gulf between the community

---

1. See in this issue Stanley Hauerwas, "Militant Peacemaking" (page 43) and Eberhard Arnold, "Beyond Pacifism" (page 31).

2. Ian Randall, *A Christian Peace Experiment: The Bruderhof Community in Britain*, 1933–1942 (Cascade Books, 2018), 18–37.

3. Emmy Barth, *An Embassy Besieged: The Story of a Christian Community in Nazi Germany* (Cascade Books, 2010), 90–93.

and the government deepened.[4] In 1934, after refusing to allow a Nazi teacher in its school, the Bruderhof started a second location outside Germany, the Alm Bruderhof in Liechtenstein, and sent all school-aged children to live there. In February 1935, on a sales trip, Alfred heard rumors of impending military conscription. Recognizing that the Nazis were unlikely to respect its beliefs, the Bruderhof decided to send all twenty-four men of military age to Liechtenstein as well. Quietly, members started collecting bicycles and obtaining passports (a delicate task). The official announcement came on March 16, 1935. Alfred and the others set out that night, making their way by bicycle and train to the Alm Bruderhof. Their wives and children (Jakob was not quite two) joined them on April 3.

Asylum in Liechtenstein was only temporary, however. Given the tiny country's size and location, Prime Minister Josef Hoop informed the Bruderhof that the government would be unable to protect German citizens for long. The Bruderhof sought yet another haven, and eventually located a farm in Ashton Keynes, England. Alfred was one of the first members dispatched to start this new venture, the Cotswold Bruderhof, in early 1936; Gretel and the children followed some months later. Germany declared conscription of citizens living overseas in January, and the German embassy began asking Liechtenstein for status updates on the Bruderhof men. But by October 3, Prime Minister Hoop was able to inform the German embassy that there were

Jakob, *left*, with his parents and siblings on the Alm Bruderhof, Liechtenstein, 1936

no more draft-eligible German men at the Alm Bruderhof; they had all escaped to England. By the end of 1937, all community members had relocated to the Cotswold Bruderhof.

The welcome they received in England was decidedly mixed. The Bruderhof connected with many members of the interwar pacifist movement, through organizations like the Peace Pledge Union. But once the Second World War broke out and anti-German sentiment spread, neighbors of the Cotswold Bruderhof concocted fabulous tales about what these new German émigrés were doing – building a submarine in their gravel pit, poisoning the Thames – and repeatedly expressed negative opinions in the local papers. The Bruderhof's pacifist stand exacerbated this xenophobia. When Britain introduced mandatory military training for young men in 1939, the Bruderhof published a statement in its magazine, *The Plough*, that "under no circumstances will any member of our communities join the fighting forces or do any alternative form of service."[5] Ultimately, all members of the Bruderhof who were called up received unconditional exemptions (remarkable considering that the British government granted only

4. See generally Thomas Nauerth, *Zeugnis, Liebe und Widerstand* (Schoeningh Ferdinand, 2017); Randall, *A Christian Peace Experiment*; E. C. H. Arnold, "The Fate of a Christian Experiment," *The Spectator* (11 June 1937), 11–12.

5. "The Brothers and Conscription," *The Plough* (Summer 1939), 61.

2,900 such exemptions during the course of the war).

It was a position bound to provoke, and to be misunderstood: many in England associated pacifism with Neville Chamberlain's appeasement policy, or even with tacit support for Nazism. Nevertheless, members of the Bruderhof endeavored to "devote all our resources to the prosecution not of war but of peace and brotherhood among men, which we feel is the best expression of gratitude we can give to this country."[6] This took practical form in varied ways, such as taking in Jewish refugee children, publishing *The Plough*, and maximizing agricultural production for the benefit of their neighbors.

The Bruderhof's stand on conscientious objection eventually forced it out of England. Letters to the local papers decried "British cowards" joining the community, and a boycott drastically reduced its income. These voices in the local and national press, and eventually in Parliament, became too strong to ignore; the Bruderhof realized the government could not afford it protection much longer. German members also lived under threat of being interned as enemy nationals. This was untenable, as the community felt it a matter of faith to remain together.

This prompted a frantic search for yet another refuge. Initial overtures to Canada were rebuffed, as well as to other Commonwealth countries such as Australia, South Africa, and Jamaica. In August 1940 two members, British attorney Guy Johnson and Swiss engineer Hans Meier, tried to secure immigration permission in the United States. With the help of a Mennonite relief organization, they were able to meet with the State Department and even First Lady Eleanor Roosevelt. But because there was no provision for group immigration and a commitment to conscientious objection was sufficient legal basis for denial of immigration, these efforts proved fruitless.

The relationship with the Mennonites, however, yielded a path forward. In the wake of World War I, the government of Paraguay, whose population had been depleted by earlier wars, had granted a group of Canadian Mennonites a blanket exemption from military service; by 1940 they, along with an influx of Mennonites fleeing Russia, had established a significant foothold in the country. While Johnson and Meier were in the United States, a Mennonite representative arranged a meeting with the Paraguayan ambassador to the United States, which led to assurances that the Bruderhof would be welcomed on similar terms. When the community in England heard that this was likely its only option, many members were apprehensive: life in a remote jungle was not what they had anticipated when they set out to be a force for peace in society.

6. "Our Members and the Tribunals," *The Plough* (Spring 1940), 30.

But they remained resolute in their determination to live out their faith as one undivided church. In November, Jakob and his family set out in the first of several groups bound for their new home.

Building Up an Alternative

Freed from the threat of conscription, the Bruderhof could focus entirely on its initial inspiration: building a community to serve its neighbors. The first project was a hospital. Over the next twenty years, it provided a wide range of services, from maternity care to surgery, for tens of thousands of Paraguayans. At the same time, the community's trained agriculturalists were applying their skills in the new environment; one successful project was breeding hybrid Zebu-Friesian cows that could produce milk in the harsh climate. In 1946, mindful of its own historical hardships, the community began a project to provide refuge for war orphans from Germany. After initial inquiries seemed positive, the community built up a separate settlement designed to care for and educate sixty children. Ultimately, the project was scuttled by the German authorities. Instead, the community used the facilities (and many members' own homes) to provide accommodation for almost twice that number of Europeans displaced by the war.

Living as committed pacifists in a society resembling the Wild West often required creativity. The young men would take turns as night watchman, walking the compound with a lantern. Besides keeping fires stoked and waking the milking crew early, the watchman had to scare off wild animals and the occasional pilferer. One member was shot in the leg upon lighting a lamp after hearing thieves outside.

The government offered little protection, due to its own instability. At the start of one revolution, Jakob found himself in Asunción, the capital city. The Bruderhof house in the city was near the naval academy and the city police station. One night, gunshots awakened the household as the naval commander led a march on the police. When Jakob ventured out the next morning, the façade of the police station was so pockmarked with bullet holes that little paint remained.

There were several such revolutions during the Bruderhof's sojourn in Paraguay. It was not uncommon that both sides requisitioned community livestock, both horses and cattle, sometimes with a promise to pay later. The community livestock manager was often dispatched to attempt to reclaim goods – nonviolently, of course. When the local commander was a neighbor, a well-timed bottle of *caña* was sometimes effective. (One time the commander thanked by offering a portion of beef off the fire, fresh from the Bruderhof's herd.) Another time, a commander agreed to return several horses but not their valuable harnesses. The Bruderhof members found their distinctive tack in a storage shed, harnessed up the horses, and thanked the commander (in front of his guests) for his generosity in returning it to them. They got away before the commander could figure how to restrain them without losing face.

Despite its remoteness, the community received a regular stream of visitors. In keeping with its commitment to live a life that transcended political and economic divisions, it welcomed guests of all stripes: Jewish refugees, wealthy Philadelphia Quakers, two brothers

> **"Under no circumstances will any member of our communities join the fighting forces or do any alternative form of service."**
> *The Plough, 1939*

In 1953, Bob and Shirley Wagoner, a couple from the Church of the Brethren, one of the historic peace churches, had visited the Paraguay community for six months. Bob, a theology student, was distressed that some eighty percent of Brethren young men had joined the military during World War II. He hoped that a recommitment to nonviolence would reinvigorate the American denomination. The Wagoners' letters home (later published as *Community in Paraguay*), raised awareness of the Bruderhof in the United States and contributed to a surge in American visitors to Paraguay.[8]

Many were conscientious objectors. In 1955 Milton Zimmerman, a young Quaker doctor from Philadelphia, was the first to obtain approval to work in the Bruderhof hospital as an alternative to military service. The Bruderhof had also opened its first US location, Woodcrest, in 1954, and many young Americans who had been conscientious objectors in World War II and the Korean War found welcome in the community. So did a number of military veterans troubled by what they had experienced in the war. This influx of enthusiastic and inspired people with new ideas invigorated Bruderhof life. Over the next eight years, the locus of the community shifted to the United States (with additional locations reestablished in postwar England and Germany). Jakob and Juliana moved to the United States in 1961.

Jakob and Juliana with two of their children, 1960

from Rhodesia bicycling around the world. Jakob spent the summer of 1955 rooming with Frederic Pryor, a visiting Oberlin student later imprisoned in East Germany and freed along with downed American U-2 pilot Francis Gary Powers in exchange for a KGB agent, as dramatized in Steven Spielberg's 2015 film *Bridge of Spies*. One Belgian family arrived with their servant Juliana Alonzo, a Paraguayan girl of indigenous Guaraní descent.[7]

Many of these visitors, including Juliana, decided to join the community. As Jakob came of age, he and many of his peers made the commitment for themselves as well. (In the Bruderhof, only adults can enter into full membership, on the basis of a free individual decision.) On one youth group outing in Paraguay's cold season, Juliana's warm-hearted nature caught Jakob's attention when she gave away her only coat to a young woman who was shivering. A friendship between the two developed, and they were married in 1957.

The American Tradition of Liberty of Conscience

Accommodation of conscientious objectors has been an issue from the beginning of

7. See "Juliana Gneiting" in Clare Stober, *Another Life Is Possible* (Plough, 2020), 26.

8. Bob and Shirley Wagoner, *Community in Paraguay* (Plough, 1991).

the American experiment. As a three-time immigrant who ultimately ended up in the United States, my grandfather would be the first to gratefully acknowledge the freedom of conscience guaranteed in this country. I thought often of his experience during a law-school seminar on the origins of the Bill of Rights. These protections were not inevitable, and still need defending today.

As early as the 1670s, several of the American colonies granted exemptions to Quakers seeking to avoid militia service.[9] Of the thirteen colonies, eleven had constitutions including a form of bill of rights, all of which included protection of some kind for an individual's right of conscience. These exemptions continued through the Revolutionary War. In 1789 George Washington, who had commanded the Continental Army, wrote to a gathering of Quakers who had expressed a desire to remain free from participation in war, "I assure you very explicitly that in my opinion the Conscientious scruples of all men should be treated with great delicacy & tenderness, and it is my wish and desire that the Laws may always be as extensively accommodated to them, as a due regard for the protection and essential interests of the nation may justify and permit."[10]

But at the same time, there were strong philosophical disagreements about conscience rights among the founders. John Locke, the English philosopher most influential on the founders' views, trusted that government would be wise enough to avoid imposing burdens on individual conscience. Though Locke advocated that people follow their consciences, he assumed they would be subject to penalties existing under the law (conscientious objection to military service was just one of several expressions of conscience at issue at the time). Among the founders, Jefferson supported this position, advocating for protecting beliefs but not necessarily actions that flow from those beliefs. Madison, meanwhile, took the more expansive view that the individual conscience was "the most sacred of all property" and ought to be accorded substantial latitude. Although Madison's initial proposal to protect "the full and equal rights of conscience" as part of the First Amendment fell victim to compromise, it was Madison's vision that substantially informed the First Amendment's protection of religion, which gradually spread to other nations.

Congress has provided explicit protection for conscientious objection ever since it enacted the first federal draft in 1864. Both the Union and the Confederacy exempted members of certain denominations from military service. During World War I, this protection applied only to members of established peace churches, such as the Church of the Brethren, Quakers, and Mennonites, and still required induction into the armed forces as noncombatants. Those who refused were subject to military imprisonment and faced other mistreatment.[11]

The World War II era saw much more emphasis on individual beliefs, rather than denominational association, in determining conscientious objector status. These men were assigned to unpaid "work of national

> "In my opinion the Conscientious scruples of all men should be treated with great delicacy & tenderness."
>
> *George Washington, 1789*

9. See generally Michael W. McConnell, "The Origins and Historical Understanding of Free Exercise of Religion," *Harvard Law Review* 103:7 (1990), 1409–1517; Mark L. Rienzi, "The Constitutional Right Not to Kill," *Emory Law Review* 62 (2012), 121–178.

10. George Washington to the Society of Quakers, October 13, 1789.

11. See e.g. Duane Stoltzfus, "The Martyrs of Alcatraz," *Plough Quarterly* 1 (Summer 2014), 36–47.

importance" in Civilian Public Service (CPS) camps, which were under the purview of the Selective Service and outside the chain of command of the military.[12] The focus on individual beliefs in conscientious objector determinations increased through the Vietnam War era. In 1965 the Supreme Court, in perhaps its most extensive examination of what constitutes "religion," broadened the statute to protect everyone holding a "sincere and meaningful belief which occupies in the life of its possessor a place parallel to that filled by the orthodox belief" in God.[13] This was later expanded further, to encompass all categorical objections to war, even if purely moral rather than religious.[14]

> ## "Our lives already are conscripted for service in another Kingdom. This is our task, our first and only loyalty."
>
> *Bruderhof statement, 1958*

Although the United States has maintained an all-volunteer military since 1972, there have been recurring calls for the return of a draft. Supporters have argued that a draft would distribute the burdens of war more equitably, and that a broader conception of national service would increase national unity. A bipartisan national commission formed in 2016 to address these concerns released its final report in early 2020. It endorsed maintaining mandatory draft registration, expanded to include women, while retaining an all-volunteer military. Recognizing the need for positive service opportunities outside the military, however, the report recommended keeping protections for conscientious objectors, and further, providing "service-year opportunities so ubiquitous that service becomes a rite of passage for millions of young adults."[15] This included proposing a tenfold expansion of federally funded national service opportunities other than the military. Currently, there are fewer than 85,000 such positions available to young people – less than four percent of the number of active duty and reserve military members. And the commission called for improving incentives to these programs such as living stipends and educational benefits; these currently lag far behind those available in the military and put these programs (such as the Peace Corps and AmeriCorps) out of the reach of many young people. These changes would go a long way toward establishing a healthy culture of altruistic national service.

Even if opportunities for national service expand, however, there will still be a need for robust conscience protection. Disputes over the right not to kill are no longer confined to the armed forces. For example, they have surfaced increasingly in the healthcare professions: pharmacies have faced regulatory inquiry for allegedly violating professional standards and nondiscrimination principles when their owners refused to supply drugs that might be abortifacients;[16] writers in peer-reviewed medical journals have argued for rules requiring doctors to participate in euthanasia in the interest of individual autonomy.[17]

Objectors to the Vietnam War

The American Bruderhof that Jakob and the other immigrants from Paraguay found on arrival had also been shaped by conscientious

12. For more background, see CivilianPublicService.org.
13. *United States* v. *Seeger*, 380 U.S. 163, 166 (1965).
14. *Welsh* v. *United States*, 398 U.S. 333 (1970).
15. *Inspired to Serve: The Final Report of the National Commission on Military, National, and Public Service*, March 2020.
16. See e.g. *Stormans, Inc.* v. *Wiesman*, 136 S. Ct. 2433 (2016) (Alito, J., dissenting from denial of certiorari); see also Brief of the Bruderhof and the National Committee for Amish Religious Freedom as Amici Curiae Supporting the Petitioners, *Stormans, Inc.* v. *Wiesman*, 136 S. Ct. 2433 (2016).
17. See e.g. Julian Savulescu and Udo Schuklenk, "Doctors Have No Right to Refuse Medical Assistance in Dying, Abortion or Contraception," *Bioethics* 31:3 (2017), 162–170.

objection. Many alumni of the Civilian Public Service camps missed the sense of comradery and shared purpose they had found there, and joined or started intentional communities; quite a few (including my wife's grandfather) eventually joined the Bruderhof. The community also befriended a wide spectrum of peace activists, from Dorothy Day to Eleanor Roosevelt.

As young men migrated from Paraguay or came of age in the United States, they too were subject to the draft. The CPS alumni were happy to mentor this new generation of conscientious objectors, through practical advice and stories. During World War II, eager to work for something positive and to demonstrate their conviction by putting their own lives on the line, many had volunteered for the most dangerous assignments. One of Jakob's new compatriots had volunteered for a smoke-jumping unit, but was rejected for being ten pounds over the weight limit. Instead, he volunteered as a medical guinea pig. Twice army doctors intentionally infected him with hepatitis as part of a study of transmission and potential treatments of the disease. Others had served as research subjects in challenge trials of early flu vaccines, receiving first the vaccine being tested, and then a dose of the virus itself.

The older objectors' advice and encouragement was invaluable, particularly for the first conscientious objectors from Paraguay. Once someone was called up, a local draft board made the initial determination whether he was sincere in his conscientious objection. Boards also had veto power over the alternative service an objector agreed to perform. (By this time,

rather than group work in CPS camps, most were assigned individual jobs with nonprofits approved as "in the national interest.") Boards were composed of local volunteers who generally had little sympathy for conscientious objectors and had a quota of men to supply the military. For Germans coming from a Spanish-speaking country, English was their second or third language, ill-suited for making nuanced arguments about personal conviction.

Nor was classification as a conscientious objector permanent. For example, when one young man obtained conscientious objector status on appeal and then attended college, Selective Service automatically changed his status to student. When he finished school, he was promptly reclassified as available for conscription, necessitating yet another (successful) appeal.

Through all this, the Bruderhof remained clear that its primary goal was living a life guided by the Sermon on the Mount. Although the community members were unanimous that they would not serve in the military, even as noncombatants, they debated what alternative service their beliefs permitted. Considering

Young men fulfill their alternative service requirements by working in *Plough*'s printshop, ca. 1967.

Jakob, *second from right*, works in the Bruderhof's furniture factory in Pennsylvania, ca. 1965.

the Brethren Service Committee. (In the end, none of the American groups saw the project to completion.) The Bruderhof ultimately had less daring activities approved as "in the national interest," including teaching in the Bruderhof's elementary schools. Work placements at Plough were also approved by the Selective Service after a rigorous vetting process confirming that Plough's purpose to "call men to turn toward God in the midst of this very needy world situation" was indeed in the national interest.

this question at a members' meeting in 1958, the Woodcrest members were clear about their priorities: "We recognize that we already have the foundation principle which is the basis for evaluating each situation of relationship to government. . . . Our lives already are conscripted for service in another Kingdom. This is our task, our first and only loyalty. We cannot heed any call or order that would take us from this task."

Eventually, the community decided to explore Bruderhof-sponsored alternative service, so young members could fulfill both obligations at once. The Bruderhof's hospital in Paraguay had already been approved, so some Bruderhof members did alternative service there until it closed in 1960. Following the example of the CPS camp veterans by seeking service that demonstrated that their opposition to war was not a result of cowardice, the Bruderhof also joined discussions about the formation of a nonviolent peacekeeping mission in North Africa under the leadership of André Trocmé and the International Fellowship of Reconciliation, in cooperation with the Mennonite Central Committee and

Jakob was never called up, so was never officially required to perform alternative service. Still, like the rest of the community, he worked to live out an alternative to war. This took many forms. Beyond the community, it included years on the local volunteer fire department squad, regular visits to the jail, and working at the food bank the community operated. Within the community, it meant being among the first at the community's workshop each morning (a habit he still maintains at age eighty-seven) while also serving the community as a pastor. For my grandmother, the most generous and loving person I know, it meant caring for her neighbors through small but practical acts of love; her well-tuned sense of the right gift at the right moment became legendary. Even while raising eight children of their own, their house was always open to visitors. It still is – not just to grandchildren, but also to young men and women seeking their own calling in life.

Beyond Resistance to War

In recent years the Bruderhof has started new communities in two countries that still have military conscription: South Korea and Austria. So young men from the Bruderhof will again be liable for military service. The similarities between these countries stop there, though, as their military regulations couldn't be more different in their implementation.

South Korea has a long tradition of military service by all male citizens – not surprisingly, given that it officially remains at war with North Korea. Military service is a cultural rite of passage, and any attempt to avoid it is highly stigmatized and could ruin one's career prospects. Until recently, the few who refused military service for religious reasons faced significant jail terms, followed by a lifetime with a criminal record. In 2018, however, the Korean Constitutional Court ruled that the country must make provision for conscientious objectors. Late last year, a group of sixty-four objectors began the first legally recognized alternative service outside the military chain of command: three years working in a correctional facility primarily as cooks and janitors. Many activists are relieved that, despite the punitive nature of the work, they have an opportunity to be of service to their country without violating their conscience.

In Austria, too, every male citizen is subject to compulsory military service. However, there is an automatic right to opt for civilian community service instead. A significant majority go this route, spending a year providing eldercare or doing environmental protection work. With these options, there is no need for special provisions to protect conscientious objectors.

Austria's universal national service suggests the untapped potential of such opportunities in the United States and other countries.

And the equitable application of conscription across society in both Austria and South Korea highlights the economic inequality of military service in the United States. The move to an all-volunteer military only accelerated an existing trend of unequal representation of the poor among military members (and resulting casualties). Beginning with near equality in World War II, each major conflict has seen a growing gulf between the average income of communities with high levels of war casualties and those with low levels.[18]

Attending high school shortly after 9/11 in one such low-income area, I was easily able to see why this inequality persisted. We lived in an impoverished county in southwestern Pennsylvania, and consensus among my classmates was that the only way to get ahead was to get out. Absent some special talent or advantaged parents, the military was an obvious path to achieving this. It was baked into the culture – the soundtrack on the school bus was militaristic country anthems such as Lee Greenwood's "God Bless the U.S.A. 2003" and Toby Keith's "American Soldier" – and reinforced by advertising on student television and at school events. Recruiters were regularly on campus, and they already had your information – if you hadn't exercised your right to opt out, buried in fine text on page thirty-three of the student handbook, along with the opt-out for corporal punishment.

> **To many of my high school classmates, the New York City that anchored 9/11 iconography was as foreign as Baghdad or Kandahar.**

18. See e.g. Douglas L. Kriner and Francis X. Shen, "Invisible Inequality: The Two Americas of Military Sacrifice," *University of Memphis Law Review* 46 (2016), 545-635.

Jakob with a grandchild, 1990

Ironically, to many of my high school classmates, the New York City that anchored 9/11 iconography was as foreign as Baghdad or Kandahar. And unlike conscripts in South Korea or Israel, the national interest they were being asked to defend was far removed from their day-to-day life. Still, whether they dreamed of traveling the world or pursuing advanced training, for many of my peers the military could feel like the default option.

In the post-9/11 environment, a return to the draft seemed possible. This gave me pause – I did not have a firm faith, but was equally skeptical of the bravado and pageantry of the military ad campaigns. It was spending time with Opa that helped me understand that it wasn't sufficient to oppose war; one must find a positive cause to advance. It wasn't so much his words as his example. He kept up an active correspondence with communities around the world. At the same time, he was deeply invested in his local community. While his firefighting days were past, his efforts at

pastoral and charitable care were redoubled. And Oma, with her quiet care for the unannounced guest and the struggling acquaintance time zones away, embodied a different version of the same commitment. In time, I came to share their quiet conviction that working toward living out the kingdom of God was a higher calling – and served one's neighbor and humanity better – than any form of patriotism.

Our society will continue to encounter questions of conscientious objection, and it would do well to learn from its history. During the Revolutionary War, the Continental Congress appealed to a charitable understanding of common purpose, rather than overzealous mandates, in its conscription decree:

> As there are some people, who, from religious principles, cannot bear arms in any case, this Congress intend no violence to their consciences, but earnestly recommend it to them, to contribute liberally in this time of universal calamity, to the relief of their distressed brethren in the several colonies, and to do all other services to their oppressed Country, which they can consistently with their religious principles.[19]

Those of us who refuse to kill would do well to learn from our own storied history, and respond in the same spirit as our forebears to this call for relief of the distressed.

When I sit with Opa now, the stories are even fewer, but he retains his verve and conviction. Our conversation is marked by stretches of deep and wise silence, the quiet confidence of a life well lived, in service to others. And I am convinced, more than ever, to follow Opa's example of living, in the words of the Quaker founder George Fox, "in the virtue of that life and power that took away the occasion of all wars." ⤳

19. Resolution of July 18, 1775, in *Journals of the Continental Congress, 1774–1789*, v. 2 (W. Ford ed., 1905), 187, 189.

Candid

Near Munich, c. 1938

Someone she loved, and who loved her, held the camera
And pointed it suddenly, teasing. The focus is blurred.
She's laughing, embarrassed and pleased, in a sun-struck meadow.
Overhead, a dark fleck in the distance might be a bird.

Whoever it was snapped the shutter before she was ready,
Her right hand half-lifted to push back the hair from her eyes
Or maybe to wave. The hands on the camera, unsteady,
Hold her like this forever, flushed with surprise.

A picnic lunch by the lake at the end of summer,
The weather not yet turned colder. Time, like a mote
In a sunbeam, floats weightless. Late sun, spilling over her shoulders,
Ignites her dark hair and the plain gold chain at her throat.

Off in the distance, late August is yielding to autumn;
Cumulus towers are brewing and brooding on rain.
There's a dark line of trees assembled along the horizon,
And farther off still, the faint smoke-smudge of a train.

Time is an album of infinite snapshots like this one,
Each page flicking open an instant. Time is untrue,
An illusion, as colors are. Put your hand through it and reach her –
A girl in a sun-bleached swimsuit that might have been blue.

CATHERINE TUFARIELLO

Editors' Picks

Charis in the World of Wonders
A Novel
Marly Youmans
(Ignatius)

Frederick Beuchner wrote, "Here is the world. Beautiful and terrible things will happen. Don't be afraid." This could be the motto for the heroine of Marly Youmans's new novel, which follows the story of Charis, a young woman whose life is riddled with unimaginable loss and undeniable beauty. Set in Puritan New England, it's a tale that will interest not just history buffs but anyone who knows the world to be a beautiful, terrible place stitched through with grace.

This is a book that does not shy away from theodicy, the reconciling of our understanding of God's goodness with the fact of evil, suffering, and chaos. In our skeptical modern world, narratives wrestling with this theme usually exist between the poles of belief and agnosticism; not so with Charis. As she seeks to make sense of her world, her first impulse is not to wonder if God exists but to look for signs of God and to wonder how God regards this world so full of peril. In a manner reminiscent of Julian of Norwich's *Revelations of Divine Love*, Charis circles around and around the problem of evil, seeking not to resolve but to confront it. With her, the reader meets horror and goodness in equal measure: massacres, witch-hunts, suicide, and freak accidents alongside the generosity of strangers, the mystery of alchemy, the comfort of scripture, the arresting beauty of nature, and the miracle of birth.

This reflects the era in which the story takes place, when people simply assumed that spiritual forces both benevolent and malevolent animated the cosmos. The most successful aspect of the book is its ability to conjure this premodern and enchanted way of encountering the world, where babies born on the Sabbath are cursed and moose are near-mythic creatures. Reading historical fiction can sometimes feel like a one-sided game of Trivial Pursuit, in which the author inflicts upon you every fact he or she ever learned about the time period. Not so with this book. Charis' world is one in which I thoroughly believed, full of people I couldn't help but care about. The archaic language felt natural, and its premodern mindset, full of assumptions alien to the modern experience, was revitalizing to inhabit.

Though masterfully researched and written with elegance and sensitivity, the narrative elements of the book fall short. Many exciting things happen, but they lack a sense of congruity, tension, or completion. At least that was the book's impression on me; I was never quite sure why I ought to keep reading, or what I was waiting for. Perhaps this narrative ambiguity is a feature of the novel, emblematic of Charis' own faltering attempts to make sense of the beauty and pain she has experienced. Perhaps we are not meant to be able to stitch the meaning of experiences together like one of Goody Holt's fine frocks, but must trust the true alchemical magic to which the heroine's name attests – a grace capable of transfiguring pain into beauty.

—*Joy Clarkson,* Plough *Contributing Editor*

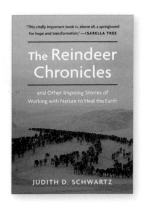

The Reindeer Chronicles

And Other Inspiring Stories of Working with Nature to Heal the Earth

Judith D. Schwartz
(Chelsea Green)

It can be hard to be an environmental optimist these days. So it's refreshing when someone reminds you that people can – and are – restoring damaged landscapes around the world. In her latest book, science journalist Judith D. Schwartz takes us around the world to visit people restoring life to the land, from the Loess Plateau in China to the rainforests of Hawaii, grasslands of eastern Washington, deserts of the Middle East and New Mexico, and the frigid Norwegian Arctic.

Along the way, Schwartz weaves the inspiring stories of her protagonists with some of their philosophy and the science and history behind what they are doing – and why it's working. Restoring carbon to the soil and reestablishing natural cycles of water in ways that return productivity to degraded land is one of the largest challenges humanity faces this century. Schwartz shows us how, working with nature, people can revitalize their land and communities through adopting regenerative approaches to farming and grazing.

In reading the book I was reminded how culture is one of the most diverse and adaptable things about humanity. It shapes how we support ourselves and work the land in ways that, in turn, impact us. Each considered on its own, the stories in *The Reindeer Chronicles* invite the reader into a unique place in the care of inspiring individuals. As a whole, they offer a visionary reminder that in restoring the world we restore ourselves, and that the key to restoring land is how we see it. Schwartz's reporting lights the way forward, helping us stay optimistic in a world that all too often seems to conspire against faith in a better future.

—David R. Montgomery, author of
Dirt *and* Growing a Revolution

I Ain't Marching Anymore

Dissenters, Deserters, and Objectors to America's Wars

Chris Lombardi
(The New Press)

In this sweeping history, veteran journalist Chris Lombardi covers people within the US military who resisted in one way or another from 1754 to 2020. Despite the scope, in some cases details are so vivid that it seems as though the author must have been a fly on the wall while events were happening.

While conscientious objection to war is an underlying element that runs throughout (Lombardi includes some of the struggles of religious pacifists during the Revolutionary War and early US history), the story she tells is much bigger than that. Much of the resistance within the military has been tied to broader struggles to establish justice and a framework for civil liberties. Conscientious objectors (COs) and war resisters of World War II later played key roles in the civil rights movement, such as Bayard Rustin, who organized the 1963 March on Washington. But this book shows how the struggle for racial justice has been deeply entwined with war resistance throughout US history.

For many reformers, it was a stint in war or the military that awakened their consciences. That holds true for well-known war resisters such as Philip Berrigan, William Kunstler, and Reality Winner, as well as for far more obscure heroes of conscience, such as Cyrus Pringle, a Civil War CO who was shackled and abused.

Lombardi highlights the vital role of veterans' organizations in this story. In the 1940s, the progressive American Veterans Committee "was hoping to shift the 'American Way' further along the path blazed by FDR, and deploy that unity and shared sacrifice in the cause of fairness and justice." Vietnam Veterans Against the War (VVAW) and Iraq Veterans Against the War (IVAW) both sponsored "Winter Soldier" hearings, in which veterans presented first-hand testimonies about atrocities including war crimes, and created guerrilla street theater to "bring the war home."

—*Bill Galvin, Counseling Director, Center on Conscience and War*

Floaters

Poems

Martín Espada
(Norton)

Martín Espada's *Floaters* captures stories of immigrants struggling against discrimination and poverty. The portraits he paints with words include Puerto Ricans in the Bronx and undocumented migrants on the US-Mexico border. Espada brings injustice to the forefront – the title refers to US Border Patrol officers' term for bodies floating in the Rio Grande – but it is his dignifying of immigrants and the disenfranchised that erupts throughout the collection with rhythmic cadences and vivid imagery.

Espada's poems lay bare the way anti-immigrant rhetoric can lead to physical violence. In "Not for Him the Fiery Lake of the False Prophet" Espada tells the story of a homeless Mexican man, Guillermo Rodríguez, who was beaten while in a sleeping bag outside a Boston subway station: "Two strangers squashed the cartilage in his nose like a can of drained beer." The perpetrators' motivation? In their own words: "Donald Trump was right. All these illegals need to be deported." Meanwhile, "Two thousand miles away, someone leaves a trail of water bottles / in the desert for the border crossing of the next Guillermo."

These poems, however, are not merely snapshots of today's political moment. They timelessly capture both sorrow and beauty, honoring those who struggle for dignity. There are love poems to the world and to a lover. In one poem Espada writes, "Then I see you, watching the violinist, his eyes shut, the Russian / composer's concerto in his head, white horsehair fraying on the bow, / and your face is bright with tears, and there it is again, the word *love*, / not a fly or a mosquito, not a cricket or a bee, but the Luna moth / we saw one night, luminous green wings knocking at the screen / on the window as if to say *I have a week to live, let me in,* and I do."

—*Sheryl Luna, author of* Pity the Drowned Horses

The Great Escape

For those trapped in the violence of poverty, rap tells heroic tales of breaking free.

ZITO MADU

I N 2002, THE RAPPER Styles P released what is his most popular and memorable song, "Good Times." The song's title is ironic, and the chorus, which features a high-pitched voice singing *I get high, high, high*, is misleading. The lyrics don't celebrate good times, nor do they celebrate smoking the weed the singer describes in detail. In fact, the song is exceedingly sad. It is full of violence and pain, the smoking a form of self-medication.

"Good Times" has stuck with me because it captures the relationship between poverty and violence so well. In three verses, Styles P clearly details how poverty is an inherently violent

I think of rappers as great American storytellers.

situation, setting the stage for individual violence as it destroys the ability to imagine other ways of being. This is a common theme in rap, but this song is startlingly honest about early death as the result of that dynamic.

Rap is fantastical; life in the songs tends to be exaggerated and extreme. In "We Gonna Make It," Jadakiss doesn't just own a fancy house – in his house his "bathtub lift up" and his "walls do a 360." And he didn't just sell drugs, he "ran through enough coke for Castro to build schools in Cuba."

Rap music and its artists have come under heavy criticism for those fantastical elements, especially when it comes to violence. Rappers are always killing hundreds of abstract enemies in songs, and buying wildly inflated numbers

of high-powered guns. The criticism has come not only from those who see rap as evidence of Black degeneracy, including the FBI, but even from more "conscious" rappers who see violence-as-entertainment as both inauthentic and a disservice to Black culture.

The latter critics have a point – this is an uncomfortable entanglement. It allows people who aren't close to Black culture to pretend that the music is a realistic depiction of American Black life. Its popularity contributes to a vicious cycle where the market demands that type of music, enriching mostly White executives, while Black artists are abandoned when the industry no longer sees them as worthwhile. Take Bobby Shmurda, who made hit songs for Epic Records, which he said reflected his real-life experiences. When he went to prison on weapons charges, the label that had profited from the underlying violence abandoned him – not before making him (literally) dance on the table for executives' amusement.

Rap has real problems, and some criticisms, of bigotry and misogyny, are valid. But I think of rappers as great American storytellers. They structure their work around rags-to-riches tales, that most American narrative of overcoming circumstance and reaching success through talent and hard work. Their stories can be heroic, too, in the exaggerated tradition of folktale, with struggles against tragic circumstance or great beasts in the form of grim conditions or implacable haters. Mariah Carey's description of Jay-Z as "the epitome of the American dream" may be applied to other great rappers: "He's been fighting all his life. He has taken his talent and his creativity

Zito Madu is a writer who was born in Nigeria, moved to the United States in 1998, and currently lives in Detroit. He's been a staff writer at the sports website SB Nation *and a contributor at* GQ.

*...rain of cash / So I could roll up, hop in the whip and like, bounce to the ave / I get, high 'cause I'm in the hood, the guns is around / It take a blunt, just to ease the pain that humble me now / And I'd rather roll somethin' up, 'cause if I'm sober dawg / I just might flip, grab my guns and hold somethin' up / I get high as a kite, I'm in the zone all alone / Muthaf*cka 'case I'm dyin' tonight / So I roll 'em up back-to-back, fat as I could / You got beef with Styles P, I come and to slide to the hood / I get high, high, high, high (Every...*

and . . . done things that are pretty much unparalleled."

But rap is more like literary fiction than pure fantasy; its monsters are real. In "Good Times," Styles P dials the fantastic down to honesty: "I get high 'cuz I'm in the hood, the guns is around / It take a blunt, just to ease the pain and humble me down," he begins. Then he leans into fantasy about the violence he could do if sober, out of frustration with his situation, "and I'd rather roll something up; 'cause if I'm sober dawg / I just might flip, grab my guns and hold something up." Life is precarious: "I get high as a kite; I'm in the zone all alone / Muthafucka case I'm dying tonight." And there's no escape: "I get as high as I could / 'Cuz if you see things, like I see things . . . I'ma die in the hood."

Tupac's metaphor for his survival was to call himself "the rose that grew from concrete." Nipsey Hussle ties the flower to self-medication on "Dedication":

Red rose in the gray pavement
Young black nigga trapped and he can't
  change it
Know he a genius, he just can't claim it
'Cause they left him no platforms to explain it
He frustrated so he get faded.

Meek Mill summarized the whole ordeal, the condition of poverty, its various traps, and the frustration of trying to escape and cope with them, in "Championships":

How could you blame me? When I'm tryna
  stay alive and just survive
and beat them odds when niggas die by
  twenty-five . . .

Tryna to smoke the pain away, they lock us up
  for smoking
Put 'em on probation, lock 'em up if you ain't
  perfect
Victims of the system like a raindrop in the
  ocean
They closin' all the schools and all the prisons
  gettin' opened.

THE POWER OF THE HEROIC TALE lies in the hope that greatness is only a matter of determination. André Gide's Oedipus, speaking in Gide's retelling of the Greek myth in *Two Legends*, captures it well:

As if I had ever sought happiness! It was to escape from it that as a boy of twenty I ran away from Polybius on my toes, with fists clenched. None can say how beautiful was the dawn above Parnassus as I went forward in the dew to hear God's oracle. I had nothing but my own strength to help me, and I didn't yet know who I was, but with all the possibilities of my being I was rich enough.

The young Oedipus sees the infinite potential of his life as a great wealth; he doesn't know that his fate is already sealed. But when all has come to pass and he blinds himself, he realizes: "Before even I was born, the trap was laid, and I could not but fall into it. For either your oracle was lying or I had no possible escape. I was caught."

Like Styles P, Oedipus is trapped, but there's an enormous difference. Before he was a king, Oedipus was a prince, by birth and adoption. His story is tragic and he suffers greatly, but when he dies, his grave is made sacred to the

gods. He was doomed, but he was pitied by the highest powers. There's no great tragedy to be written of a young Black kid who doesn't survive. As Meek Mill says, he's a raindrop in the ocean.

For Black Americans, the violence of poverty can't be disentangled from the racism of history. All the way through life, indignity is made worse by bigotry, with gross inequalities built into the education, housing, finance, healthcare, policing, and carceral systems, and more.

The coronavirus pandemic has disproportionately devastated Black communities. In a late 2020 piece for the *Atlantic*, Ed Yong explains why, going back to the thwarted Reconstruction era through the present day to show how Black Americans have been repeatedly, intentionally, and structurally denied access to healthcare. On top of existing disparities, this vulnerability means that Black Americans have been dying of Covid-19 at "a rate more than twice that of white Americans. That figure is both tragic and wholly expected given the mountain of medical disadvantages that Black people face." There are those who shrug all this off – in America, where individual responsibility is the great myth, weakness is held as a sign of personal or collective failing. This notion is intertwined with the national deflection of the effects of racism and White supremacy, and how that ideology still shapes society.

It's often argued that elevated rates of poverty and violence are evidence of a corrosive culture. In a 2017 essay arguing against this idea, Jamelle Bouie cited sociologist Patrick Sharkey, who found that "relative to whites, African Americans of all income and educational levels have seen a remarkable amount of downward mobility over the last forty years." Sharkey also found that "even if a white and a black child are raised by parents who have similar jobs, similar levels of education, and similar aspirations for their children, the rigid segregation of urban neighborhoods means that the black child will be raised in a residential environment with higher poverty, fewer resources, poorer schools, and more violence than that of the white child."

Khalil Gibran Muhammad tackled that same argument in his *New York Times* review of *A Peculiar Indifference: The Neglected Toll of Violence on Black America* by Elliott Currie. Muhammad takes the dynamic that rappers point out – that systematized injustice is a sort of violation that leads to individual violence – and shows how it's flipped in the racist assumption that violence is naturally inherent in Black people:

> White domination rests at the center of this maelstrom of enduring and endemic violence. And yet, whether most white Americans admit it or not, they consider Black people both the deserving victims and the dangerous vectors of violence, who bear the burden and the blame for much of the nation's exceptional record of death and destruction.

The trap of being Black and poor is designed into the system. It is worse than a trap laid by far-off gods, as it is laid by other humans. Dignity is stripped from those who find themselves born into it and there is no distinction even in death.

Oedipus might imagine infinite possibility, since the world seems open to him until the end of his life, but someone like Styles P knows much better about the path before him. With cruelty as the accepted order of things, the countless people who fall victim to it barely register; if anything, they are blamed for their condition to begin with. Those who don't survive are simply raindrops in the ocean.

MOST OF MY TIME listening to rap as a teenager was during the morning drives when my father took me to one school and my siblings to another – Cass Tech, the most prestigious public high school in Detroit, whose students had to pass an entrance exam and maintain a 3.0 GPA. Fighting meant expulsion. I lasted just a year at Cass before moving on to Northwestern, where I was among the mass of average children from the city, poor Black children of poor parents.

When I went from Cass to Northwestern, it upset my parents and was a source of familial shame. But these days I tell them that I am grateful for that fall into the general population. At Northwestern, I felt more at home than I did at Cass; I was able to see how the frustrations of poverty and being trapped in a limited life led to outbursts of violence. I saw how hard teachers, principals, and counselors worked to save as many as they could, fighting against so many inequalities of resources, and how easily children could fall behind and be disregarded as unsalvageable. My friends whom I loved.

Northwestern was dangerous. There were fights, shootings, drinking, unsafe sex, police officers constantly circulating outside and inside the school, and occasionally actual deaths. There was fun and joy as well, but ever-present tension, especially because I knew the kids there as full people with ambitions and baggage which limited them. The trap was no more escapable for being clearly visible.

Rap music that comes out of this background acts as a platform for grief; it's survivor's remorse music. In the same albums where rappers are talking about violence, multiple cars, women, guns, and their endless money, they're also mourning. Styles P eulogizes his younger brother: "Life is a circle of pain / The darkest clouds end up like the purplest rain / They say patience is a virtue in the game / Fuck it, I guess I died when my brother died."

In "Love My Life" Cam'ron pays homage to his cousin who died in 1997. Biggie Smalls dedicated the song "Miss U" to a friend he was trying to help escape the drug game who was killed instead. Nipsey Hussle himself was shot and killed in 2019 and has been eulogized in numerous rap songs. Dr. Dre dedicated "The Message" to his brother, Tyree Du Sean Crayon, who was killed in a street fight. One of the most iconic rap songs, "They Reminisce Over You (T.R.O.Y.)" by Pete Rock and CL Smooth, was inspired by the death of their close friend, Troy Dixon. In "Life Goes On," Tupac eulogizes numerous friends who died or went to jail, saying, "But now that you're gone, I'm in the zone / Thinking I don't wanna die all alone, but now you gone / And all I got left are stinkin' memories."

The list could go on forever. Rap is filled with songs about relatives and friends who have died or disappeared into jails, and because the rappers tend to understand the role luck played in their own escapes, they feel they could still fall victim to the same violence. Styles P's paranoia that he will die in the hood is a shared anxiety in rap.

A FEW YEARS AGO, I wrote about Malcolm, a friend of mine from Northwestern. In twelfth grade, when I had grown out of fighting and had the possibility of going to college and being more than I had imagined, I asked him if maybe he should do the same. He knew, he told me, that he was going to die doing what he was doing. And he did.

I have the same sadness for my own friend that I have when I hear "Good Times" by Styles P. Not just that I wish each of them saw beyond the world that poverty had given them, but also that what they said could be false. The worst thing about their declarations isn't that they're fatalistic or self-fulfilling, but that from all the consequences of poverty and racism, and how our society is structured and who it is built to crush, what they said is generally true.

Along with the grief of survivor's guilt, I also instinctively understand the extreme

hedonism. It's as if those who didn't imagine they could make it, and then do, are intoxicated by that great escape – going from limited life to an overindulgence of it. But beyond the fantastical, there is a joy that comes from seeing friends who make it – who live lives that outside the context of poverty would be considered commonplace.

A year ago, I was a groomsman at my best friend's wedding in Kingsport, Tennessee. We hadn't seen each other in a long time. He now works as an engineer and has a nice lake house, car, and boat. As I gave my toast after the wedding, I was so overjoyed by the deceptively mundane things that he was experiencing. That he could go to work, go home, watch movies with his wife, and live comfortably enough to never worry whether the money he has will be enough, or if he will be a victim of random violence, makes me very happy.

And sometimes I check up on Styles P on social media to see how he's enjoying life. He has a few juice bars around New York, still makes music, and often talks about health and fitness. It seems very ordinary, far from the

There is a joy that comes from seeing friends who make it – who live lives that outside the context of poverty would be considered commonplace.

extreme hedonism and success that his own lyrics talk about, but it is its own wonder, at a great distance from the limits ordinarily set on a poor Black individual.

Nothing will be solved by exceptions: for each one who makes it, there are many more who don't. Still it is always wonderful to see the ones who manage to escape, to see them get to a place of stability and comfort. Knowing where they came from makes even the most banal things, like Styles P taking walks in nature and doing videos about healthy eating, seem actually magical. The ordinary magic of waves lapping at the shore. ✈

back, fat as I could / You got beef with Styles P, I come and to slide to the hood / I get high, high, high

RACHEL PIEH JONES

Call to Prayer, Call to Bread

What the Five Pillars of Islam Have Taught Me

Eighteen years among Somali Muslims in the Horn of Africa have taught an American Christian that Islam's five pillars apply to Christianity as well. In this excerpt from a new Plough book, *Pillars*, she describes what she has learned about one of these five pillars, prayer.

Call to Prayer

I had expected mornings in Borama to be quiet. No traffic noise, no refrigerator humming, no fans whirring, no airplanes overhead. But sounds of Somalian village life swept in through our screened windows before the sun even peeked over the mountains. A rooster crowed, and next door a woman chanted and sang. I went out on the veranda and, over the walls surrounding our house, watched the singing neighbor gather brown eggs. A cart dripping water rattled past, pulled by a weary-looking donkey guided by a man slapping its hind legs. A fight broke out between stray dogs among the cacti and thorn bushes across the dirt road. With a high-pitched yelp, a female limped away from the pack.

These were not sounds of machines or mass productivity but of life: water, animals, singing. Over the cacophony came the deep, clear song of the muezzin, reminding faithful Muslims that prayer is better than sleep.

"Allahu Akbar! Allahu Akbar!" God is great!

An American living in Pakistan said once that when she heard this call to prayer, the *adhan*, she would rush to cover her infant's ears so the devil wouldn't get inside the baby, or turn on loud Christian praise and worship music to drown the sound of evil. Another woman told me the Islamic call to prayer terrified her and led her to pray against the enemy. I think she meant Muslims.

This is how some Christians respond to Islam: it can contain nothing good and should be feared or defeated. This is also, I would learn, how some Muslims respond to Christianity: ready to argue, quick to believe misconceptions, primed for violence. Thomas Merton said people are "cutting themselves off from other people and building a barrier of contrast and distinction." I cannot shake one of his next sentences: "And thus I spend my life admiring the distance between you and me."

Women and children who fled Al-Shabaab Islamists wait in line at a feeding center in Mogadishu, Somalia

---

Rachel Pieh Jones has written for the New York Times, Christian Science Monitor, Huffington Post, Runners World, *and* Christianity Today *from Djibouti, where she and her husband run a school. Get her latest book,* Pillars, *at* Plough.com/Pillars.

I wasn't afraid, hearing the *adhan* that morning. I felt no blanket of darkness settle over me and felt no urge to cover my twin toddlers' ears or pray about "enemies." Rather than admiring the distance between Muslims and myself, or building a barrier of contrast, I felt compelled to step toward God – and in doing so, step toward my new Muslim neighbors. There was an immediate hunger for participation. The sense that I wasn't part of Islam, that this call to prayer was not calling *me*, only increased that hunger.

Salat, the second of Islam's five pillars, governs Muslims' daily lives. Five times a day, men gather at the mosque and women pull prayer rugs from closets. Why? I wondered. What was the man behind the speaker saying? How many of my neighbors responded to his call? Did it feel like a joy or a burden? Or both? How did they experience God in those moments? Was that the only way Muslims prayed?

Maybe interfaith dialogue starts with curiosity.

I loved watching Somalis pray. I still do, though it can feel awkward to stare into the bubble of holy space they create any and everywhere – airports, market stalls, hospital corridors, beaches, track and field competitions. I've learned not to walk in front of someone praying, but all other motion and conversation continues around them.

Muslim men are encouraged to pray at the mosque, but other than on Fridays, women most often pray at home. They time the prayer around a pot of rice, around playdates and birthday parties. Toddlers crawl over their mothers' prostrated backs; older children bounce babies. Human life and spiritual life, tangled up together.

After washing, Muslims turn toward the Kaaba in Mecca, Saudi Arabia, and silently declare *niyyah*, their intention to focus on God.

I watched as women whispered the prayers under their breath. They tucked their toes into the material of their long dresses and pulled scarves over their heads like clouds, like Moses hidden in the cleft of the rock so the presence of God could pass by. They sat back on their heels and ran one finger along each knuckle, reciting the names of God.

Then, finished, they would abruptly return to whatever task they'd set aside.

Pray without Ceasing

I spent all my free time studying Somali, even though another American told me that every foreigner she knew who spoke Somali got killed. She also told me every foreigner who wore Somali clothes got killed. Later, I recognized her warnings as concern stemming from trauma, from losing people she loved while working in southern Somalia – but the message wasn't very encouraging.

The afternoon call to prayer became my signal to cover my head and go outside. It meant the indoor morning work – washing clothes by hand, preparing rice and goat for lunch, dusting floors – was over, for me and for my neighbors. It meant the afternoon siesta was over too, and the sun would set in less than three hours. It was time for *shirshir*, visiting.

I loved that afternoon call to prayer, because it released me from my morning isolation, from being cooped up with the twins and Somali language textbooks. Afternoons became my opportunity to humiliate myself as I stumbled through conversations and tried to develop relationships with the women on our street, tried to find or create common ground.

I remember one such conversation with a neighbor. We were in the dirt road between our houses, and our children played with stones

and thorn bushes nearby. The sun was setting and the *maghrib* call to prayer sounded from the mosque across the street, ending the social visiting. She called her children to go into the house so she could pray.

"Do you pray?" she asked.

"Yes," I said.

"When do you pray?"

"All day."

She looked at me like I was either a child or an alien. I knew I had said the words correctly. She sighed and went into the house. At the time I felt a sense of victory. I'd had a conversation! In Somali!

Now I know why she looked at me that way. I was both a child and an alien. Infantile in my understanding of prayer, Islam, my own faith, and the Somali language. And a foreigner – with a culture so completely other, I may as well have landed in a UFO and sprouted a tail.

She had used the word *salat*, ritual prayer. It would be physically impossible to pray the *salat* all day. Spontaneous prayer, *du'a*, carries less value than the required *salat* among most

Muslims. *Du'a* was more like what I did when I prayed for a parking spot.

When I told my neighbor I prayed all day, I was clearly a liar. I wasn't bowing and kneeling that moment in the street. She saw me in the market, buying watermelon by the slice and meat from fly-ridden slabs, not bowing or kneeling. When she asked if I prayed, I not only gave an answer that made no sense in her worldview, it wasn't true in mine; I certainly didn't pray all day.

I initially felt proud about this short conversation. I thought I had, in just a few words, explained something meaningful about Christians, and prayer, and how we're so devoted that we don't limit it to five times a day – about an intimate and ongoing relationship with God. Again with the competition and pride. I had desired to set myself not alongside but apart, even above.

I watched my neighbor pick up a water bucket from her courtyard for her washing, then turned to call the twins home. She would pray. She would beat a fresh batch of *laxoox*, spongy fermented flatbread, for the next day's

Fudima Ali, twelve, takes part in a basic education program.

Children collecting water at an IDP camp near the Mogadishu airport

breakfast. She would turn on the radio and listen to BBC Somali.

At my house, we would spread jelly on baguettes and sing songs, to the background whine of mosquitoes. The twins would be asleep in an hour, and I would burn popcorn and watch a movie with Tom, our nightly ritual. There was nothing else to do after dark, since we weren't supposed to leave the house.

But I couldn't let go of the conversation. All these years later, I puzzle over it. What was I trying to communicate? What did she understand? I was quick to proclaim a depth of spirituality I lacked, and I didn't see it as deceit but as conviction, as rightness. Now that I speak Somali better, I wish I could go back to that Somaliland neighbor. I'd like to hear her articulate what prayer means to her beyond the little I could understand in those first months. I'd like to know what she experiences when she prays. I'd like to ask if she feels God's presence, if she finds rest on her knees, or how she overcomes apathy when it flattens her spiritual life. I'd like to tell her how I recognized God in our long-ago conversation, because she was willing to put up with the strange foreigner who spoke like an infant and tripped over her

own dress and didn't belong there, in the dirt street between our houses.

Call to Bread

The call to prayer woke me my first morning in Somaliland, and the call to bread woke me the first morning in Djibouti, less than a year later. I didn't know it was a call to bread. I thought it was a bird dying and making an awful spectacle of it.

Insistent honking echoed through our home again at noon, four, six, and eight o'clock. For a full week I thought birds died in Djibouti at regular intervals every day, until I discovered not belly-up bird carcasses, but the bread man.

Every neighborhood had several bread men, and every bread man pushed a wooden cart with a horn strapped to the handle. The honking horns announced the arrival of fresh baguettes. The bread man strode up and down each street. He paused on corners, or outside houses with predictable bread needs, and honked. A single delicious baguette, crusty on the outside with a center of spongy fluff, cost twenty-five Djiboutian francs. Thirteen cents.

At the sound of the horn, children scurried from behind curtained doorways or towers of discarded tires, clutching precious coins in tight fists. Guards outside gated middle-class homes stepped over makeshift beds of flattened cardboard to purchase baguettes – for their parents, for their employers, for their own bellies, which grumbled on cue when the bread man appeared around the corner.

I'd expected the *adhan* to dictate the rhythm of life in this, my second Muslim country; I had not been prepared for the bread man. The call to prayer was at once unifying and divisive. Muslims around the globe bowed the knee and brushed their foreheads against the ground. For me, on lonely days, it was a reminder five times a day that I was an outsider, that I didn't belong, that sometimes I wasn't wanted. But the call to bread reached all our ears with the same demand. Come, eat, bite into a toasty baguette, and be satisfied. It reminded me of our shared humanity, inspiring me to consider how I might reinterpret the call to prayer for myself.

The Quran teaches that God scattered *ayat*, or signs, everywhere throughout the earth, to point to God, to turn humans toward worship. "And in your creation, and what he scattered through the earth of moving creatures, are signs for people who have faith with certainty" (45:4). I started to see the call to prayer and the call to bread as two of these signs, turning me toward God and toward neighbor.

Prayer times, roughly corresponding to bread times, occur at sunrise, midday, mid-afternoon, sunset, and between sunset and midnight. Each crackling buzz over the neighborhood speakers was a sign. Even before the muezzin began his call, the community knew it was time. For me, time to seek out more sacred signs of God. For Muslims, time to remember God, time to wash, *wudu*.

Washing the body, for my Muslim friends, wasn't an empty ritual, though some confessed

it felt that way at times (turns out Christians aren't the only ones to struggle with feelings of dullness). But the forced pause in activity provided opportunity to focus single-mindedly on Allah.

Could I, a Christian, view *wudu* as another sign of God at work? Humans, taking an extra moment from a busy day to remind themselves of their distance from holiness, to embody faith by washing dirt from the flesh.

None of my Somali friends believed the water washed away their sins. Washing is done in obedience, in a moment of vulnerable spirituality – with damp sleeves and beads of water dripping from the chin. Their focus was on earning God's favor and forgiveness by meticulously following the rules, though there is no guarantee. Muslims are in a liminal state, on the threshold between the physical and spiritual. They hope their prayers will be accepted, that God will pour out mercy.

The water dripping from foreheads and staining knees, the bruises, the timing, the call, are not only about obedience. They designate people of faith. The call to prayer is a loud (sometimes fuzzy or crackling) interruption of the day. I needed to be interrupted, disturbed. It is too easy to go about daily life ignoring the signs, without taking a moment to stop and turn to God.

In the evenings, I strained to hear the bread man's horn before he turned up our street, so I would have time to find twenty-five francs. Night falls fast this close to the equator, and darkness had swallowed up shadows, long and narrow, by the time the bread man arrived. This was a ritual I could enter, joining my neighbors on the street.

Tomorrow, these rituals would begin again. Call to prayer, honking bread delivery. Come, pray. Come, eat. ⮑

Bread and Wine
Readings for Lent and Easter

Dietrich Bonhoeffer, Dorothy Day, Søren Kierkegaard, C. S. Lewis, Philip Yancey, Eberhard Arnold, Fyodor Dostoyevsky, George MacDonald, Henri J. M. Nouwen, Sadhu Sundar Singh, Thomas Merton, N. T. Wright, William Willimon, and others

Culled from the wealth of twenty centuries, these accessible selections are ecumenical in scope, and represent the best classic and contemporary Christian writers.

Publishers Weekly: Has there ever been a more hard-hitting, beautifully written, theologically inclusive anthology of writings for Lent and Easter? It's doubtful.

Hardcover, 430 pages, $24.00

Easter Stories
Classic Tales for the Holy Season

C. S. Lewis, Elizabeth Goudge, Leo Tolstoy, Jane Tyson Clement, Alan Paton, Oscar Wilde, Ruth Sawyer, Anton Chekhov, Selma Lagerlöf, Claire Huchet Bishop, and others

A treasury of read-aloud tales selected for their spiritual value and literary integrity.

National Catholic Register: This thoughtfully curated collection is remarkable for its range and breadth. . . . Keep the book close and pull it out whenever you and your family need a reminder of the great Easter themes of transformation, reconciliation, and the triumph of life over death.

Softcover, 383 pages, $18.00

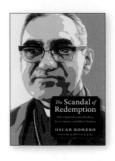

The Scandal of Redemption
When God Liberates the Poor, Saves Sinners, and Heals Nations

*Oscar Romero
Introduction by Michael Lapsley*

A modern martyr lifts up the poor, provokes the powerful, and invites each of us to walk with him.

Pope Francis: Archbishop Romero invites us to sanity and reflection, to respect for life and harmony.

Henri J. M. Nouwen: Romero does not speak from a distance. He does not hide his fears, his brokenness, his hesitations. It is as if he puts his arm around my shoulder and slowly walks with me. He shares my struggles. There is a warmth in his words that opens my heart to listen.

Softcover, 139 pages, $12.00

The Crucified Is My Love
Morning and Evening Devotions for the Holy Season of Lent

Johann Ernst von Holst

Handed down for generations, these stirring readings for every day of the Lenten season spring from a pastor's heart. Expanding on the Gospel accounts, they draw the reader into deep contemplation of Christ's suffering, accompanying him in vivid detail on his last journey from Bethany to Golgotha.

Softcover, 329 pages, $18.00

All books 40% off for *Plough Quarterly* subscribers. Use code PQ40 at checkout.

Poetry You Can Touch

An Interview with Rhina P. Espaillat

This year, *Plough* is launching a new poetry competition, the Rhina
Espaillat Poetry Award. *Plough*'s poetry editor A. M. Juster spoke
the poet, who recently turned eighty-nine. >>

I remember little incidents – the young woman who was looking after my cousin George and me told us that we mustn't play with the Black children. I told that to my father and he said, "Oh, did she? Well, I'll have a talk with her." So he did and she never did anything of that kind again. Because of course we are a mixed people – to have your children told that you mustn't play with people who are part of your family!

Your father and your great-uncle had fled the Dominican Republic because they had stood up to Trujillo.

It was not as simple as that. They were in Washington, DC, for diplomatic dealings for the Dominican Republic, which owed money to the United States. My great-uncle was there as an emissary, not ambassador – he was a *ministro*, a servant of the state.

It was during autumn 1937, when the killing of the Haitians in the Dominican Republic took place – between 18,000 and 20,000 people on the border lost their lives. Trujillo sent what was really his private army. It was the police and other civil forces, but he had turned them into his private army, and they did whatever they were told, so they were killing people who had lived on the border for generations.

They were as Dominican as I was, but he had an anti-Black thing. His mother was Haitian – I think he had all kinds of complexes.

Left: Rhina P. Espaillat's parents in Central Park, New York, 1947

Right: Her green card photo, 1939

A. M. Juster: About ten years ago, you and your late husband Alfred came to visit Laura and me in Washington, DC. We went to the World War II memorial, which had just opened, for Alfred, because he fought in the Battle of the Bulge. We also walked up Sixteenth Street, where you lived for a while as a very small child.

Rhina P. Espaillat: It meant a lot to me, that visit. I was very grateful to you both for taking me there because I always wanted to see that house. I was only, I think, three at the time, and my only clear memory of Washington is of standing up in the back seat of my great-uncle's car, looking out the oval window and seeing the Washington Monument retreating in the distance.

Rhina P. Espaillat *was born in the Dominican Republic and came to the United States as a young girl, settling in New York City. As a bilingual poet, Espaillat is winner of numerous prizes including the T. S. Eliot Prize, the Richard Wilbur Award, and (twice) the Howard Nemerov Sonnet award. Her most recent book is* Brief Accident of Light: Poems of Newburyport, *a collaboration with poet Alfred Nicol, with illustrations by artist Kate Sullivan (Kelsay Books, 2019).*

A. M. Juster *is a poet, translator, and essayist, and* Plough's *poetry editor. He worked in senior positions for four US presidents, including twice in the White House and as Commissioner of Social Security. His most recent book is* Wonder and Wrath *(Paul Dry Books, 2020); he is currently working on a translation of Petrarch's* Canzoniere.

La Magdalena responde a quien juzga con dureza

Si juzgar es lo que gozas,
explícame—y sé sincero—
tu motivo verdadero:
¿Es tildarme de asquerosa?
¿O enseñar a ser virtuosa
la infeliz de mala fama
que se usa y no se ama?
¿O te engrandece humillar—
y en público despreciar—
la que gozas en la cama?

Dicen que en Belén nació
un hombre bueno, apacible—
con piedad hacia el falible:
sostiene al que tropezó
y levanta al que cayó.
Dicen que es buen consejero
ese joven carpintero,
porque conoce el dolor,
sabe juzgar con amor,
y es más tierno que severo.

RHINA P. ESPAILLAT

Mary Magdalen Responds to the Harsh Judge

Be honest, please: I long to know
why judging others makes you glad:
does my uncleanness make you sad,
or lift you high as I am low?
Do you intend to heal the bad?
Or is it, rather, your delight
to humiliate and slight
those who are used and spoken of
with cruel contempt and never love,
though they may well please you by night?

I've heard a man from Bethlehem—
a man of peace, both good and humble—
steadies the fallible who stumble,
and if they fall he raises them,
rather than scornfully condemn.
Because he has known pain and fear,
that youthful carpenter holds dear
not just the virtuous but the rest;
at love and counsel both, the best,
by far more tender than severe.

RHINA P. ESPAILLAT

He was a very complicated, very sick man. He wanted to erase the Black from us. Also, it was a handy thing, like the Jews for Hitler, handy and very convenient. He would say to the Dominicans, "Of course we're having economic trouble because these people are coming over the border."

But my father and my great-uncle didn't flee the Dominican Republic – they were already in the United States at the time. When the massacre happened, my great-uncle said, "I'm finished." When he showed my father the letter he had written to the Dominican government, my father said to him, "You know what this means, you know what is going to happen" – he would lose his government post, and not be allowed back. He said, "Yes, but sometimes you have to do what you have to do." He was a brave man, a good man.

From there you went to New York City?

Yes, because they were in Washington with just what was in their valises. That's all they had. They had no job. They had no place to live because the place on Sixteenth Street was not our home anymore.

My mother did a really crazy thing. She took me back to the DR because she had lost

The poet in carnival costume, Dominican Republic, 1938

a child as a result of the stress and the misery of being exiled. She was very sick; she thought she would never see her mother again. Back in the Dominican Republic she collected her sewing machine because she knew she'd have to earn a living in New York, and then she went back to New York, leaving me with my father's mother for close to two years.

My father and great-uncle meanwhile found an apartment and got jobs – not very glorious ones, but they paid the rent. By the time they sent for me, they had sort of a life. I came in the spring of 1939; I thought it was freezing.

You were attending high school in Manhattan when you had your first poems published, in Ladies Home Journal, *then went on to study at Hunter and Queens College before becoming a teacher in New York City schools. What was it like teaching poetry in a public school classroom? Was it difficult to get your students to engage with particular poets?*

No, as a matter of fact I found it easy. I had trouble with the boys sometimes; they would put their hands in front of them and say, "No, no, no, no. I don't do poetry." I always said, "Yes, you do. You just don't *know* that you do." I found out that the way to teach New York kids is to make them laugh.

They loved *The Iliad* and *The Odyssey* because I used to act out the parts. Once I was doing Helen visiting the walls of Troy so that the Trojans could see her. I was sitting on the edge of the desk and saying "the armies were looking up at her, and the old men of Troy were looking up at her. Then she took off the veil." With that, I leapt off the corner of the desk and landed with both feet in the wastebasket. That went over very well.

I can imagine!

The thing is to make them feel that this is not so sacred that it can't be touched by human hands. You have to make poetry theirs, and you make it theirs by bringing them into that life. I told it with a little trimming of gossip. "Can you imagine what the servants thought when their boss Menelaus was not there? This handsome young man from Troy comes in and stays with the queen. What do you think?"

But in addition to that, you have to do the psychology of that story, the wonderful ways in which Homer lets you know that they are soldiers but they are afraid of death. Homer wants us to feel for the soldier who was not a Greek but a Trojan, so the enemy is human, and that's so important.

One of your most popular poems is called "Bilingual/Bilingüe." Could you tell about its inspiration and evolution?

That poem came out of reality in the apartment of my parents, where I was permitted to speak English outside the door, but not inside; my father wanted me to be bilingual. He said, "She's got to be part of the world, so Spanish in here, English out there." I used to come home from school and say, "Let me tell you what the teacher said today," and he would say, "*No, no, mi hija, dímelo en español, en castellano.*" I would say, "I want to tell you exactly the way she said it," but he was very firm. At home that was sacred – I had to speak Spanish.

So "Bilingual/Bilingüe" sort of fell together – it had to have a little Spanish in each of the couplets, but by the end the Spanish no longer has parentheses around it: by that time we're joined in it.

Joined in it – that's right. You've translated Richard Wilbur and Robert Frost into Spanish; are there other poets you've done or are planning on doing?

Hazme, vida, quizás tu pregonera

Hazme, vida, quizás tu pregonera
de elogios, como elogian la mañana
el olor a café y la luz temprana;
o más íntima aún, tu camarera,
para asearte, y servirte la primera
taza del dia, y abrirte la ventana
para que veas la tierra, tan lozana
y fresca como tú. Qué gusto fuera

agradecerte así que me trajiste
al mundo a conocerte; me brindaste
sonidos y sabores; me vestiste

de carne que a tantos les negaste;
y por un tiempo—o, generosa fuiste!—
qué incomparable amante me prestaste.

RHINA P. ESPAILLAT

The Widow Offers Herself to Life

Make me your herald, Life: send me ahead
to hail you, as the earliest light is doing
for each day, and the scent of coffee brewing.
Or—cozier still—make me your maid instead,
to serve your coffee, wash you, fresh from bed,
dress you, and part the curtains for your viewing
of the earth, as young and constantly renewing
itself as you. What joy! Let it be said—

my gratitude!—to you, who opened wide
the world to me; who saw fit to present me
with sound and taste; you by whom I was dressed

in flesh, which to so many is denied;
and for a time—oh, generous!—made blessed
with the one and only lover that you lent me.

RHINA P. ESPAILLAT

An idea cooking in my head is a book of two poets, Emily Dickinson and Sor Juana Inés de la Cruz, because for me they are the first two great poets of the continent. Those two women for me are the most innovative, the most daring, and maybe the most skilled of the beginning of this double continent.

I've also done Edward Taylor and George Herbert. It's interesting that I gravitate toward the religious poems – the poems in which somebody extremely bright either argues with God, or pretends to argue with God, or does something unexpected rather than saying, "You're perfect, you're perfect, you're perfect," which is boring. I like the way Herbert deals with God because he said, "I slammed the table. I said, no more, that's it. I've had it with you!" That's wonderful.

Tell people about Sor Juana.

Sor Juana is one of my saints. I adore her because she was so daring, so smart. In seventeenth-century Mexico, it was not a good idea for a woman to be that smart because she was surrounded by guys who thought that women should have a place in the kitchen. She didn't want the kitchen. She became a nun not because she had a tremendously powerful calling, but because she wanted her privacy. She wrote a great many religious pieces that are outstanding, and she did her duties as a nun, of course. But she also wrote the most passionate love poetry.

She wrote Latin poetry too, which is much harder to compose because the prosody is so different.

With a cousin in New York City, 1939

But she did it. What's more, she even wrote poems in Nahuatl. She studied philosophy and music and science; she was far ahead of her time.

The Inquisition got so annoyed with her that it sent word through one of the archbishops that she had better be very careful because she was becoming vain – by that they meant she published her poetry. They frightened her and said, "The only way you are going to get through this safely is to get rid of your scientific instruments and all your books."

So she got rid of everything. She got into her old clothes, took care of sick nuns, then promptly got sick herself and died in her forties.

The other Cruz is Saint John of the Cross, Juan de la Cruz, and I adore him. What he did was to write, quite literally, love letters to God because in his poems he becomes the soul, which of course has to be female. The soul in his poems is always a woman very much in love with her husband who misses him all of a sudden. It's absolutely enchanting.

What else are you working on now?

I have also been working on Gerard Manley Hopkins, because I adore him.

I would think Hopkins would be very difficult to get into Spanish.

Very.

Dickinson too. Her vocabulary is so unusual, I wouldn't know how to…

I can deal with vocabulary. The trouble with her is you have to fracture the syntax. You can't write smoothly the way you would write a Frost translation. I have to make it slightly twisted and crooked the way she is in English.

The year 2020 was in so many ways a bizarre time. What's given you grief and what's given you joy this past year?

What's given me joy is the same thing that always gives me joy: I have a wonderful family, a wonderful collection of friends, a collection of poets who are like family.

What makes me wretched is that there are 650 children or so who were separated from their parents at the US-Mexico border and may never see their parents again – that I find heartbreaking. I go to bed every night thinking about that because I lived for two years without my parents. I was in my grandmother's house surrounded by wonderful old people who were my relatives, but I missed my parents just the same. So I can imagine what the children are going through; it breaks my heart.

Many other things trouble me also, such as the amazingly huge distance between the very rich and the very poor. In the richest, most fortunate, and best country in the world that should not be happening.

Let's talk about the poetry award that Plough created in your honor, to recognize poems reflecting your "lyricism, empathy, and ability to find grace in everyday events of life." The judges' job is to select those poems that reflect the values and the work of Rhina P. Espaillat. What qualities should they look for?

What's important for me is important to *Plough*. They defend everybody. They will speak for the Israelis. They speak for the Palestinians. They speak even for people who have gotten into trouble. They believe, as I do, that we are all one family. That's Christianity for me. ⤳

This interview from December 22, 2020, has been edited for clarity and concision.

A Backward Look

The perfect girls our Mamas meant to rear
seldom appear,

or never, now. Back in my time, wherever
some clever

daughter mouthed off in public, or defied
the social guide,

or thought she could—with arguments!—debate
her elders, fate,

Mama took her aside, not to upset her,
but teach her better:

Be quiet. Sit. Don't make me say it twice.
Prickly advice.

Some of us turned out much like Mama, though
a silent "No!"

crept into every dialogue, and kept
some secrets swept

into dark corners. But, different altogether,
sons prospered, whether

they matched a pattern set by father, mother,
or chose some other—

all by themselves!—from the adventurings
of ruthless kings,

or buccaneers, or gods from pagan days,
with Papa's praise

and Mama's pride. Everybody enjoys
rearing their boys.

Do they break things, mess up, fight, swear and spit?
Get over it.

RHINA P. ESPAILLAT

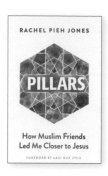

Pillars
How Muslim Friends
Led Me Closer to Jesus

*Rachel Pieh Jones
Foreword by Abdi Nor Iftin*

Personal friendships with Somali Muslims overcome the prejudices and expand the faith of a typical American Evangelical Christian living in the Horn of Africa.

Marilyn R. Gardner, *Between Worlds:* As an American raised in a Muslim country, I have waited for a book like *Pillars* all my adult life, a personal book that discovers similarities and honors differences between Christianity and Islam, a book that, pillar by pillar, builds bridges of greater understanding across what are often chasms of disconnect.

Softcover, 280 pages, $17.99

Freiheit!
The White Rose
Graphic Novel

Andrea Grosso Ciponte

The dramatic true story of a handful of students who resisted the Nazis and paid with their lives, now in a stunning graphic novel.

Forbes: Ciponte . . . adopts a cinematic pace for the story, allowing it to unspool through the ordinary moments in the lives of the five protagonists. In doing so, he gives the characters depth and dimension beyond their historical role as resistance martyrs. *Freiheit!* is an important reminder that the darkest times can't extinguish the spark of human conscience.

Hardcover, 112 pages, $24.00

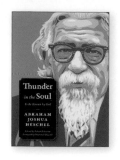

Thunder in the Soul
To Be Known by God

*Abraham Joshua Heschel
Edited by Robert Frlewine
Introduction by Susannah Heschel*

Like the Hebrew prophets before him, the great American rabbi and civil rights leader reveals God's concern for this world and each of us.

Publishers Weekly: Illuminating. . . . Those new to Heschel will appreciate this accessible introduction.

Softcover, 168 pages, $12.00

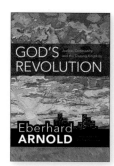

God's Revolution
Justice, Community, and the Coming Kingdom

*Eberhard Arnold
Introduction by Stanley Hauerwas*

A radical vision for a society transformed by the teachings and spirit of Jesus.

Juli Loesch: The undeniable power of Arnold's writing owes to the fact that there is no difference between what he professed to believe and the way he lived. It gives his words a resonance and depth, a right to be heard.

Thomas Merton: Arnold's writing has all the simple, luminous, direct vision into things that I have come to associate with his name. It has the authentic ring of a truly evangelical Christianity and moves me deeply. It stirs to repentance and renewal.

Hardcover, 232 pages, $20.00

All books 40% off for *Plough Quarterly* subscribers. Use code PQ40 at checkout.

THE
MINIMALIST

A Boxing Story

SPRINGS TOLEDO

I USED TO BOX IN MY SOCKS. I couldn't afford boxing shoes and I learned the hard way that pivoting around the ring in sneakers gets your ankle twisted, so I boxed in my socks. There was another reason, more philosophical, that made it feel right. My approach to the sport began with the notion that it isn't a sport at all, that it's a rawboned collision of the oldest kind and there's no need for superfluities. To my way of thinking, such things belonged in more communal, mainstream sports where they chase balls in regulation regalia or run around on a field loaded up like storm troopers. In the bloody ring, superfluities only distract from the point. In the bloody ring, less is more.

The boxing room at the Huntington Avenue YMCA in Boston, Massachusetts, was located, appropriately, in the basement. The directions you got at the front desk called to mind Wes Craven's first horror film, "last room on the left." It was a grimy, uninviting place and civilians steered clear of it. There was no climate control, no windows. In the winter it was an icebox, in the summer an oven. At the back of the room, beyond the benches and the bags, was the bloody ring.

Three days a week I'd come in for sparring sessions, a Mike Tyson minimalist stripped down more than anyone else, as if I didn't give a damn, as if I wasn't afraid. Tyson did away with robe and socks. I wouldn't wear shoes or even a cup until a friend offered an old Ringside groin protector that was held together by stink. I spurned headgear; I'd complain to the trainers that I couldn't see hooks coming in.

They had protocols of safety, however, and they'd slap it over my head anyway and yank the straps so tight I couldn't hear much else besides my own breathing, which got heavier by the minute – which presented another problem. After about the fourth round, wheezing filled my ears, scrambling my internal dialogue and transforming the headgear into a padded panic room.

But the trainers left by eight and their safety protocols left with them. Rogue trainers came in later and set up smokers, usually five- or ten-rounders with no regard for weight classes, much less headgear. Some of the roughest characters in Boston would swagger in and often stagger out. The smart ones stayed out of the ring. Smarter still were the ones who came in wearing their excuse: "Man, I would, but I'm dressed to the nines!"

There was a ragtag band of regulars. Among them was an Italian from East Boston who hit me so hard the lint flew off my socks. There was Barry, who was a great inside fighter because he couldn't see past his arms and had to be. There was Marathon Man, whose prominent nose was bent against the cushioned bar in the middle of his Face-Saver headgear when I slammed an overhand right into said cushioned bar, which snapped said prominent nose.

Stonewall Strickland was standing nearby when that happened. Six-foot-two with a build that gave him his name, he was something else altogether. Marathon Man was bleeding all over the canvas and trainers were scrambling

Springs Toledo is a freelance writer of literary nonfiction and the author of Smokestack Lightning, Murderers' Row, In the Cheap Seats, *and* The Gods of War. *His work has been featured on NPR's* Here & Now, *recognized dozens of times by the BWAA, and honored in* The Best American Essays 2019 *and* 2020. *He is currently working on a book about the Boston underworld.*

for towels when I climbed out of the ring and saw Strickland staring blankly ahead, his gloves inert at his side.

I'd heard whispers that he'd stabbed his father to death during an argument. It made the *Boston Globe* and Strickland did time for it. Then I heard it was his younger brother who killed his father, and that he took the rap. He was a haunted man.

He could bench-press well over four hundred pounds. I didn't buy it then any more than you do now until I saw it with my own eyes. Strickland was hoisting it up and bringing it down without even a grunt, like it was nothing.

I stuck around after my fight to watch his against a six-foot-five cruiserweight named Tyrone Smith. He fought him as if it was Smith who'd killed his father. "I'll beat Strickland," I, a middleweight, said at the end of it, while a sweat-drenched Smith hugged Strickland and Strickland stared blankly over his shoulder. "I'll beat him," I said again. Someone heard me and extended the courtesy of a warning. "You

know he never holds back, right?" I didn't care. I figured if you beat Godzilla, you become Godzilla. And "Godzilla Toledo" sounded good to me.

I got my chance soon enough and found out early that Strickland was too strong to fight inside. He was shifting me off balance and lighting me up whenever he felt like it, so I moved further away and fought him just outside his reach, inviting his punches and then sliding under and around them, throwing counters as hard as I could. I was watching for superfluities, knowing that if I fell for a feint or a stutter step he'd knock me stupid.

I was still watching for superfluities when he stepped in with the least superfluous attack in boxing: a jab followed by a straight right hand, the old one-two. I parried the jab and rode the right by turning my left shoulder and shifting my weight onto my back foot. He threw another one-two and I did the same thing – parried the jab, rode out the right hand. He saw the pattern and set me up. He threw the jab again, which I predictably parried, but

I FIGURED IF YOU
BEAT GODZILLA, YOU
BECOME GODZILLA.
AND "GODZILLA
TOLEDO" SOUNDED
GOOD TO ME.

he waited a second before throwing the right hand. So I was riding out what hadn't come yet and when I came back looking for it, I found it. It exploded on my chin. I didn't feel a thing. Everything went black and quite blissful, actually. Witnesses laughed when they told me that the force of Strickland's punch bent me over backwards, that my left leg shot up and I became a human seesaw with my head nearly touching the canvas behind me and my sock hovering somewhere around Strickland's nose. When I seesawed back, my sock smacked the wet canvas and I began fighting like a desperado. That's what they told me, at least.

In the locker room afterward, Strickland admitted to someone something I somehow missed: that I'd had him out on his feet in the third round. I wish that someone hadn't told me that something; somehow it makes me feel like a coulda-been. I coulda been holding my head up instead of in my hands all the way home on the Orange Line. I coulda been Godzilla Toledo.

Strickland turned professional in the cruiserweight division and had his first – and as it turned out, his last – bout. It was a decision win over a 0–5 fighter called Spider Gilchrist at an armory in Stoughton.

And then tragedy struck again. It happened because Strickland was safeguarding the Roxbury Boys Club where he volunteered,

because he escorted a gangbanger out of the building one day and the gangbanger returned with friends and baseball bats. Strickland knocked a few of them stupid but they swarmed him. He lost teeth, suffered a broken nose, and his skull was noticeably dented at the upper left corner of his forehead.

After that he had a tough time holding a job – paranoia set in and trouble followed.

One winter morning I got a collect call from the Nashua Street Jail, just around the bend from the site of the Charles Street Jail where he'd been held years earlier as a suspect in his father's murder. The voice on the other end was gravelly and to the point. "Can you bail me out?"

He was on crutches and wearing hospital pants stained with his own blood when I got him. He told me he'd been homeless for some time, that all of his worldly possessions were in the tote bag he carried everywhere he went. "Less is more," he shrugged. On cold nights, he'd been breaking into Boston University buildings to sleep in basements as grimy and uninviting as that basement gym at the YMCA.

"You're no burglar," I said. "How do you get in?"

"I pull on the door and break the dead bolt."

That's what he was doing the night before when the police appeared; he was pulling on a door. He was trying to walk away when they came at him for the second time. One of the officers took a swing at him with a nightstick, and Strickland took it away from him, tossed it aside, and began running away for their sake more than his. A cruiser sped up and struck him, sending him airborne on Commonwealth Avenue.

I drove him to Fontaine's and ordered us a couple of chicken baskets. "I owe you," he said and we sat in silence until he excused himself and hobbled to the men's room. He'd been gone fifteen minutes and I was watching the

men's room door when a sudden fear gripped me and I ran over and barged in. Stonewall Strickland was standing in the stall on his crutches, sobbing.

That was over ten years ago. He stopped calling, but not before he paid me back in full, dismissing my protests in the name of self-respect. Eventually, I gave up driving around Boston looking for him, though I still slow down if I happen to glimpse a towering black figure walking alone down a byway or carrying a tote. He may prefer not to be found.

I still see his name now and then on police blotters, stealing fruit from supermarkets, breaking and entering, trespassing. Not too long ago, the owner of an apartment building in Brookline told police he'd been sleeping in the basement for a week. I can't imagine what he sees when he closes his eyes or what he feels when roused by the brightening sky and the sound of early morning traffic. He was twenty when his father was killed that early May morning in 1988. I read the coverage in the *Globe* and came away with haunting,

shutter-shock images of Strickland, hunched over his father in a futile effort to administer first aid; standing off in Boston City Hospital as he is pronounced dead; driving around in a daze until blue lights surround him; staring blankly in a raucous courtroom, a statue in a storm, while his lawyer tells the judge something that bothers me to this day: "We don't know what really happened."

"He was a good kid," his uncle told the *Globe* back then. "He wasn't into drugs or thuggery or anything bad. He was a young man trying to make something out of himself."

He did make something out of himself. Proof of it is in that tote bag he carries everywhere he goes. Inside, underneath his few scant articles of clothing, is an old VHS tape of the Spider Gilchrist fight – proof that he was once a professional fighter, a *winning* professional fighter with a zero at the end of his record no smaller than the zero at the end of Rocky Marciano's or Floyd Mayweather's.

The details are superfluous, and only distract from the point. ⤳

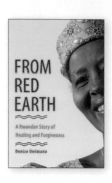

From Red Earth
A Rwandan Story of Healing and Forgiveness

Denise Uwimana

As men with bloody machetes ransacked her home, Denise Uwimana gave birth to her third son. She and her children survived the 1994 genocide; her husband and other family members were not as lucky. If this were only a memoir of those chilling days and the long, hard road to personal healing, it would be remarkable enough. But Denise Uwimana didn't stop there. She has devoted her life to empowering other genocide widows to band together and rebuild their lives.

Softcover, 220 pages, $18.00

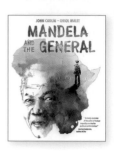

Mandela and the General

John Carlin; Oriol Malet

The struggle for racial justice will be won when we win over our adversaries. Find out how Nelson Mandela convinced a white nationalist leader to call off his militias in this graphic novel.

Library Journal: A fascinating parable with relevance to today's polarized politics.

Foreword Reviews: Excellent . . . a well-told, perceptive view of both sides in the conflict.

Softcover, 112 pages, $19.95

Why Forgive?

Johann Christoph Arnold
Foreword by Steven McDonald

Arnold lets the untidy experiences of ordinary people speak for themselves – people who have earned the right to talk about forgiving.

Booklist: A most impressive book. . . . so powerful that tears often impede reading.

Houston Chronicle: Thought-provoking and soul-challenging. . . . Arnold writes with an eye-opening simplicity that zings the heart.

Softcover, 232 pages, $12.00

Seeking Peace
Notes and Conversations along the Way

Johann Christoph Arnold
Foreword by Madeleine L'Engle

There is a peace greater than self-fulfillment, a peace greater than nations no longer at war. But it will demand a relentless pursuit kept up only by hope and courage, vision and commitment.

Jonathan Kozol: A tough, transcendent envisioning of peace. Arnold writes in the tradition of the Berrigans, of Simone Weil and Thomas Merton.

Softcover, 254 pages, $12.00

All books 40% off for *Plough Quarterly* subscribers. Use code PQ40 at checkout.

(continued from page 120)

new babies refused to baptize the infants; their consciences would not permit them to do so.

Zwingli called for a public disputation, a debate between himself and his erstwhile fellow translator. On January 17, 1525, the debate took place. The town council declared Zwingli the victor. Manz might not have disagreed: despite his language study, his education was not in the kind of dazzling humanist rhetoric that Zwingli had mastered, nor was his theology as sophisticated. But his conscience, informed by the words he had himself read, could not budge. The council ordered Felix and his group to baptize their unbaptized infants within eight days. Instead, the little group gathered a few days later at Anna's house – and baptized each other.

Days later, Georg Blaurock, who had come to Zurich to hear the disputation and had been convinced by Felix, interrupted the state church service, standing to speak about the doctrines of the *Täufer*, the baptizers. The following day, the little circle was raided. Most of the group were arrested and fined. Some paid the fine. Felix, asserting that the city had no jurisdiction over the group of believers, refused, and was for the first time imprisoned.

By spring of that year, Felix was back out and preaching again, somehow having managed a prison break. He was eventually taken up again, but released when he vowed to stop preaching – a vow he promptly broke. The next two years saw the movement grow, despite a new mandate against adult baptism, with violations punishable by death. Finally, on December 3, 1526, Felix and Georg, preaching together, were taken up again.

Georg was sentenced to banishment. Felix, unlike Georg a citizen, was sentenced to death. He did not dispute the charges; he would even then, he said, not refuse anyone baptism, if

they were willing to be instructed in the faith. On January 5, 1527, he was led from the prison to a little skiff, preaching to the gathered townspeople as he went. Anna called encouragement to him from the bank of the Limmat. Out in midstream, a pole was run between his bound arms and legs. Those on the bank heard him sing, his voice echoing back toward Anna's and up to the skies: "*In manus tuas, Domine, commendo spiritum meum.*" And then he was pressed into the river, held beneath the water until he drowned.

"Only love to God through Christ shall stand and prevail," he wrote during his last few days in that cell, in a letter to the *Täufer*, "not boasting, denouncing or threatening. It is love alone that is pleasing to God; he that cannot show love shall not stand in the sight of God. The true love of Christ shall not destroy the enemy; he that would be an heir with Christ is taught that he must be merciful, as the Father in heaven is merciful."

Born out of wedlock, Manz never married, and his travels seem to have taken him no further afield than the outskirts of Zurich. But his conviction that his whole life must be one of obedience to the gospel, as he understood it by his own encounter with the Word of God, led him to become one of the founders of a community that was a radically new way of understanding what Christian commitment means, and then to a death which was the spark of the Radical Reformation. ⤳

An illustration from the official account of Felix Manz's execution; Felix is on the platform, and Anna is somewhere in the crowd.

Felix Manz

SUSANNAH BLACK

With Artwork by Jason Landsel

ON JANUARY 21, 1525, a group of fifteen or so friends, mostly young men in their early twenties, gathered at the Zurich house of Anna Manz. What they were there to do was not yet technically illegal, but it soon would be. Georg Blaurock went first: he made his confession of faith, and Conrad Grebel baptized him. The others, one by one, made their confessions; Blaurock baptized them. The first church of the Radical Reformation was formed.

Felix Manz, Anna's son in his mid-twenties, was one of their number. Two years later and five hundred yards away from her house, he would die, drowned in the Limmat River by order of the city fathers.

It had started some years before, in 1519, when a new priest was called to the church in Zurich: Ulrich Zwingli, a scholar and powerful preacher whose exegetical sermons to the people of the city were also passionate calls for them to submit their lives to the Word of God. Felix was drawn to Zwingli's project: the reform of the Catholic Church – and a translation of the whole Bible into German. The young man, who had a thorough knowledge of Latin, Greek, and Hebrew, became Zwingli's disciple, fellow-worker, and friend.

But he found, as the two men's work of translation and exegesis went on, that his convictions and Zwingli's were no longer in harmony. Zwingli's reforms, he was convinced, did not go far enough: the church, as Felix understood it from the Scriptures, could not be an organization linked to any earthly government; still less could it come under the jurisdiction of the city fathers of Zurich. Moreover, Zwingli called for the baptism of infants to continue as it had when the church of Zurich had been fully following the understanding of Rome. But baptism, Felix was convinced, was a sign of commitment following an adult conversion, a profession of belief, not to be imposed on children who could not yet make such a profession. There was more: Christians, he believed, must not bear the sword nor hold state office; the Christian community must be one in which, at the very least, wealth is shared freely with those in need.

Zwingli continued his controversial preaching. But in 1523, Manz, along with his friend Conrad Grebel, began speaking as well, making their own converts to this more radical way of understanding what Christian commitment meant. Dangerously, several couples with

> For the first Anabaptists in 1525, nonviolence was what separated the church from the world.

(continued on preceding page)

Susannah Black *is an editor of* Plough *and has written for* First Things, Fare Forward, Front Porch Republic, Mere Orthodoxy, *and the* American Conservative. *She lives in New York City.*
Jason Landsel *is the artist for* Plough's *"Forerunners" series, including the painting opposite.*